More Praise for Awakening My Heart

"Andrea Miller is one of contemporary Buddhism's most original and arresting voices. *Awakening My Heart* has that rare combination of insight and empathy that distinguishes the very best spiritual literature. It is an inspiring, expansive, and probing exploration of what it means to be alive and practicing the dharma today."
— Shozan Jack Haubner, author of *Zen Confidential*

"A natural reporter, Andrea Miller is a keen listener and an astute observer — not only of the subjects of her reporting but also of her own mind, and that's what you want in a contemplative journalist. These lovely pieces span a huge, eclectic range from rock stars and actors to gurus and birds. There is joy in these pages, and the stories here will cause you to love life, and people, all the more."
— Barry Boyce, Editor-in-Chief, *Mindful* magazine

"This book is a concise, witty, and intelligible way to understand Buddhism."
— bell hooks, author of *All About Love*

"I love the way Andrea Miller weaves her personal experience and memories into reporting on these carefully curated subjects. I am lying on the yoga mat with her at the Thich Nhat Hanh retreat, listening to Gina Sharpe at New York Insight, and sitting in the Four Seasons with Bernie Glassman and the Dude (what a treasure!). *Awakening My Heart* is a journey of precious dharma moments, grounded in these great teachers. Thank you! I read most of these articles and interviews in the magazine, but loved them even more here, together, because they inform each other and enrich the whole intersectional story."
— Mirabai Bush, author of *Walking Each Other Home*

"In meaningful interaction, there should not exist a hierarchy, only mindful conversation and an openness to the possibility of change. *Awakening My Heart* speaks to the core of this. *Lion's Roar* editor Andrea Miller has not only interviewed some the wisest Buddhist practitioners in the world, but also Buddhist celebrities, like Tina Turner, and she does it in a way that de-centers the ego. What comes forth from her essays and interviews is shared beauty, wisdom, and at times, essential vulnerability. Miller is an extraordinary writer, unafraid to expose that which hurts and heals — like the heart."
— Ira Sukrungruang, author of *Buddha's Dog & Other Meditations*

Awakening My Heart

Articles, Essays and Interviews
on the Buddhist Life

Andrea Miller

Pottersfield Press, Lawrencetown Beach, Nova Scotia, Canada

Library and Archives Canada Cataloguing in Publication

Title: Awakening my heart : essays, articles and interviews on the Buddhist life / Andrea Miller.
Names: Miller, Andrea (Shambhala sun editor)
Identifiers: Canadiana (print) 2019011973X | Canadiana (ebook) 20190121238 | ISBN 9781988286884 (softcover) | ISBN 9781988286891 (EPUB)
Subjects: LCSH: Religious life—Buddhism. | LCSH: Spiritual life—Buddhism. | LCSH: Buddhists—Religious life. | LCSH: Buddhism. | LCSH: Buddhists—Interviews.
Classification: LCC BQ5395 .M55 2019 | DDC 294.3/444—dc23

Cover design: Gail LeBlanc

Back cover author photo: Liza Matthews

Pottersfield Press gratefully acknowledges the financial support of the Government of Canada for our publishing activities. We also acknowledge the support of the Canada Council for the Arts and the Province of Nova Scotia which has assisted us to develop and promote our creative industries for the benefit of all Nova Scotians.

Pottersfield Press
248 Leslie Road
East Lawrencetown, Nova Scotia, Canada, B2Z 1T4
Website: www.PottersfieldPress.com
To order, phone 1-800-NIMBUS9 (1-800-646-2879) www.nimbus.ca

Printed in Canada
Pottersfield Press is committed to preserving the environment and the appropriate harvesting of trees and has printed this book on Forest Stewardship Council® certified paper.

Conseil des arts du Canada Canada Council for the Arts

NOVA SCOTIA
NOUVELLE-ÉCOSSE

NOVA SCOTIA

Funded by the Government of Canada

Financé par le gouvernement du Canada

Canadä

MIX
Paper from responsible sources
FSC® C103567

For Mum and Ron

Contents

Introduction

At first blush, Buddhism didn't appeal to me. I was twenty years old when introduced to the foundations of Buddhist thought and, for me at least, that was too young to appreciate the dour note on which the Buddha's teachings begin.

The thing is, I wanted my spiritual life to be wrapped in ecstasy – or at least exuberance – and the other traditions I was familiar with seemed to have more of a knack for tapping into that. As I saw it, Christianity belted out its gloriously good news; Hinduism was a roaring party with all the most fascinating, colorful gods in attendance; and paganism was a deliciously earthy mix of wine, sex, and walking barefoot in the woods. So I compared all those sacred pleasures with the foundational teachings of Buddhism, the four noble truths, and I quickly looked away.

There is suffering. That is what I didn't want to see. And that, according to the Buddha, is the first noble truth. Sometimes our suffering is extreme, but more often it is simply the nagging dissatisfaction we feel with our always imperfect world. When we don't get what we want – *exactly what we want* – we suffer. Yet we also suffer even when life hands us what we crave. Usually it's because, a week or a day or an hour later, we decide we want something else, something more. Sometimes it's because, after we get what we want, we lose it or we live in fear of losing it.

When I encountered the four noble truths for a second time, I wasn't yet thirty years old. Not so much time had passed, but it was enough. I'd begun to notice how the mind works, how life works – the pattern of it – and I saw that it was true. There *is* suffering. Though that wasn't the love-and-light message I'd wanted, once I sat with it for a while, I realized that acknowledging the first noble truth isn't pessimistic; it's realistic. Suffering, or *dukkha*, is simply the way it is. Moreover, the truths don't end there.

The second noble truth pinpoints why we suffer, that is, we suffer because we're so stuck on what we want and don't want, what we like and don't like. The problem isn't enjoying things, people, and experiences; we can and should fully relish the exquisite pleasure of a scrumptious risotto or our child's soft, messy kiss. But the only thing that will really give us lasting happiness is if we don't cling to that enjoyment – if we let it come and let it go. Of course, the tricky part is actually being able to do that.

Buddhism's good news, the third noble truth, is that it really is possible to stop clinging and end suffering. Then the fourth noble truth is the recipe for making it happen, the eightfold path: wise view, wise intention, wise speech, wise action, wise livelihood, wise effort, wise mindfulness, and wise concentration. In a nutshell, enlightenment is rooted in developing wisdom, living ethically, and meditating.

I say this about enlightenment as if I know what I'm talking about, but believe me, I don't. No one is mistaking me for a buddha; I'm not even a very good Buddhist. I was recently asked about my morning practice and had to confess that I don't have one. Each a.m., I'm just trying to survive getting me and the kids dressed and out the door.

But what I do know is that even with my lackadaisical practice, Buddhism has given me a few more tools. The first time I truly realized the power of meditation I was on a long flight. I'm normally a nervous flyer during takeoff, landing, and turbulence, so much so in fact that I often find myself grabbing the arm of whoever happens to be sitting beside me. This one time, though, I decided to meditate simply because I'd finished my book. Twenty or thirty minutes later, we hit a rough patch and, while many other passengers seemed alarmed, I stayed effortlessly calm. I didn't even realize until the plane was flying smoothly again that this was unusual for me.

In a similar way, mindfulness has helped me to be more patient in the face of annoyance, to be more accepting of change, and to deeply savor all sorts of ordinary joys, from the sight of

a yellow leaf cartwheeling across the lawn on a windy day, to the sound of hot water pouring from a kettle, to the feel of my husband's hand in mine.

I had understood "there is suffering" to mean "there is always suffering," but that's not it at all. There is joy, too. And it is so much sweeter, so much more poignant because it is fleeting and because it is so wrapped up in this imperfect world. As Leonard Cohen put it, "There is a crack in everything. That's how the light gets in."

I'd like to thank all the wise and fascinating people I've interviewed over the years. Though not all of you are in this book, you have all enriched my life. I also want to thank *Lion's Roar*, especially editor-in-chief Melvin McLeod and publisher Ben Moore. The material in this book was originally published on the magazine's pages, and they generously gave me permission to collect it here in this form. Finally, I'd like to thank a couple of people in my personal life. Thank you to Rachel for being such a very good friend to me for so many years and, now, such an equally good *tía* for my kids, and thank you to my husband Adán Cano Cabrera for everything. Our life together is my greatest joy.

The Dude and the Zen Master

The Bromance of Jeff Bridges and Bernie Glassman

I.n the parlance of our times, Oscar-winning actor Jeff Bridges and Zen teacher Bernie Glassman have a bromance. For more than a decade, they've been smoking cigars and shooting the shit together – like the time Roshi Bernie suggested that Jeff's famed character, the Dude, might actually be some sort of Zen master, and Jeff responded simply, "What the fuck are you talkin' 'bout, man?"

Now a slice of their freewheeling exchange has been published in book form as *The Dude and the Zen Master*.

To talk about this new release, I requested an interview and today is the day. The three of us are settling into a corner of the lounge at New York's Four Seasons Hotel and Bridges is asking if photos will be taken during our conversation. If so, he wants to set a good example and put away the water bottles an assistant has provided for us. "I'm trying to get off these plastic things," he says. Three water goblets quickly appear on our table, plus a Danish and coffee with milk for Glassman and, for Bridges, tuna tartare, which is prettily served with pine nuts and chilies. As for me, I resist the urge to bring up white Russians – the drink of choice for the Dude, the character Bridges played in *The Big Lebowski* and for which he's earned a cult following.

When I ask Glassman what initially drew him to Bridges, he says, "Jeff is well-known, but he's just a regular guy. He's not somebody who makes himself out to be more special than anybody else. He's interested in serious subjects. He's comical and open. A lot of people only want to talk about their thing, in their way, whether it's the liberal cause is the only cause, or some other cause is the only cause, or you've got to be Buddhist or you've got to be Zen or Tibetan. Everybody's got so many fixed opinions

– opinions they fixate on. I found Jeff to be much more open."
For his part, Bridges says he was drawn to Glassman from the
get-go because he defied his expectations of a Zen master. With
him there was no formality, no big deal.

Before Bernie Glassman was a Zen master, he was an engi-
neer and mathematician working in the aerospace industry. As he
sees it, it was not a big leap from that field to Zen, because Zen
is all of life. In everything we do, we can bring to bear what, in
The Dude and the Zen Master, he calls "the Zen of action, of living
freely in the world without causing harm, of relieving our own
suffering and the suffering of others."

Glassman did his Zen training with the legendary Zen
master Maezumi Roshi, who played an instrumental role in establishing genuine Zen in the West. They met in 1963, when
Maezumi was a young monk assisting an old roshi at a Zen temple in Little Tokyo, Los Angeles. Glassman asked the old roshi
why they punctuated their sitting practice with walking meditation. But the roshi's English was poor, so he indicated that
Maezumi should respond. "When we walk, we just walk," was all
Maezumi said. That, according to Glassman, was the beginning:
he wanted to "hang with this guy."

A few years later Glassman was Maezumi Roshi's right-hand
man and – as Glassman puts it – he was traveling with Maezumi
wherever he went and getting to meet "all the old-timers," the
pioneering Buddhist teachers who came West. Glassman chose
to stay with Maezumi Roshi because – in his opinion – Maezumi
had a very clear understanding of the dharma. "Now," says
Glassman, "I look back and think, who the hell was I at that age
to be able to judge who had a clear understanding? It's more
accurate to say that I liked the way he talked about the dharma."

"Maezumi Roshi was in a way a very soft person and in a
way a very dogmatic person," Glassman continues. "In our private studies, he'd always tell me that he was Japanese and could
not make an American Zen. But he could help me grasp the

essence of Zen and I should swallow it all up and then spit out what didn't work for me. In fact, when I was ready to go start my own center, he said, 'I'll stay away for a year because I don't want to influence you.'" Maezumi's desire for Glassman to create his own way stood in curious contrast to his rigid emphasis on linear hierarchy. The teacher-student relationship is clearly defined in traditional Japanese culture, says Glassman. "You can't be a friend to somebody who's studying with you." So his relationship with Maezumi was imbued with this formality. "At the same time," asserts Glassman, "we were so close that the boundary moved," even though the words didn't.

Glassman still remembers when Maezumi told him that he was planning to make him a roshi, and Glassman said he didn't want to use that title. "What do you mean?" asked Maezumi. "What do you want to use?" Bernie, just Bernie, was the answer. But that was a no-go for Maezumi, so Glassman relented: "roshi" would be fine. "I couldn't have hair when I was with Maezumi Roshi and I couldn't be Bernie," says Glassman. "Then he died in '95, and by '96 I was Bernie again, and I had a beard and hair." For Glassman, this marked a shift away from the traditional, linear hierarchy of student and teacher. Maybe he's a little further along on the path than his students, but he believes that – hanging with them – they're all learning together.

Jeff Bridges played his first film role when he was six months old, an uncredited part in the 1951 release *The Company She Keeps*. By nature he was a happy baby, but his part required him to cry. "Just give him a little pinch," his mother suggested. "So that," Bridges laughs, "was the beginning of my acting career."

Bridges describes himself as "Buddhistly bent." As often as he can, he does sitting meditation for twenty minutes in the mornings and he reads the dharma, especially the teachings of Chögyam Trungpa Rinpoche and Pema Chödrön. He says he's particularly into *lojong*, a Mahayana system of mind training, and is curious about the Kagyu lineage of Vajrayana Buddhism, sometimes called "the mishap lineage" and renowned for some outrageous characters who rejected the saintly stereotypes. Paraphrasing Pema Chödrön, Bridges says that "when you pay homage to these cats, whom people could think of as very flawed," you're paying homage to that side of yourself as well, accepting the full package of who you are. Like all of us, they started out as confused, mixed-up people, and yet – by never giving up on themselves – they ultimately discovered their own genuine quality, their buddhanature.

According to Bridges, when he meditates he often makes small adjustments to get back into the space of simply being, and as an actor he does the same thing. He plays a scene one way, then another, and each time he makes an adjustment he clicks into a new space – the space of the present moment.

As a kid, Bridges practiced his acting skills with his father, Lloyd Bridges, the well-known star of *Sea Hunt*, a high-adventure television series that was syndicated for decades. In *The Dude and the Zen Master*, Bridges recounted, "If we were doing a scene together, he'd say, 'Don't just wait for my mouth to stop talking before you answer. Listen to what I'm saying and let that inform how you talk back. If I say things one way, you're going to react one way, and if I say them a different way, you're going to react a different way.' Or he'd give me this direction: 'Make it seem like it's happening for the first time.'" In Zen that's called beginner's mind.

Recently, Bridges worked on the supernatural cop film *R.I.P.D.*, and just before beginning a scene his costar Kevin Bacon would state gravely: "Remember, everything depends on this!" Because the filming was so clearly not a life-and-death situation, this would make everyone laugh and peel away the tension. But, according to Bridges, there was a grain of truth in what Bacon said. in a sense, everything does depend on just this moment.

Bridges' late mother, Dorothy Bridges (née Simpson), played a great role in informing his spirituality. While he was growing up, she had him and his siblings read *The Daily Word* over breakfast. These teachings come from the contemplative Christian tradition, but when she was around ninety years old, she turned to Buddhism, and Bridges remembers taking her to a Buddhist talk. After the teacher had finished speaking he invited questions, and Dorothy raised her hand. "Words, words, words!" she shouted when she was called upon. "Yes, exactly," the teacher responded.

But Dorothy had a lifelong passion for words, both reading them and writing them. Once, when asked if there was anyone she'd ever been in love with before her husband, she sighed, "Only my English teachers."

Lloyd and Dorothy's first child, Beau, was born two days after Pearl Harbor and had to be delivered by candlelight because of a power blackout. In 1948, Garrett followed, but when he was less than two months old, he died of sudden infant death syndrome. According to Dorothy, it's commonly believed that children are our immortality, but they're really closer to our mortality; we love our children more than we love ourselves and yet we can find ourselves powerless to protect them. Nonetheless, she and her husband went on to have two more children: Jeff, born in 1949, and Lucinda, born six years later.

Young Jeff sometimes appeared in *Sea Hunt*, and one day he was on the set when a director yelled at an underling. Bridges says, "My dad went up to the director and very calmly said to him, 'I'm going to be in my dressing room in my trailer. When you're ready to apologize to this guy in front of all of the rest of us, that's where you'll find me.' So the guy had to apologize."

The young Bridges was mortified, yet ultimately grew up to admire his father's sense of justice and love of acting. "He really enjoyed the communal aspect of everybody working together to pull off a kind of magic trick," Bridges says. "He would create a joyful atmosphere that was contagious. That relaxed people, and out of relaxation comes the cool stuff. A lot of folks in showbiz don't want their kids to go into it because it's got a dark side.

But my dad encouraged all of us. He would say to me, 'Jeff, do you want to come to work with Dad? Come on, you'll get out of school! You can make some money, buy some toys!'"

Bridges, however, resisted becoming an actor; it felt to him like nepotism. He wanted to be appreciated for his own talents, not because his famous father was opening doors for him. Yet there was nothing to worry about. With the release of Peter Bogdanovich's seminal 1971 film, *The Last Picture Show*, everyone knew that Jeff Bridges was a talent in his own right. He earned his first Oscar nomination for his role and ever since he's had a steady career, playing in one or more movies most years and earning five more Oscar nominations. He was up for Best Supporting Actor for both 1974's *Thunderbolt and Lightfoot* and 2000's *The Contender*, while 1984's *Starman*, 2009's *Crazy Heart*, and 2010's *True Grit* got him nominated for best actor. many people consider his win for *Crazy Heart* to be a long-overdue acknowledgement of his remarkable career.

I was on the subway in New York, preparing for my Bridges and Glassman interview by reading *The Big Lebowski and Philosophy*, which is part of the Blackwell Philosophy and Pop-Culture series. Suddenly, the guy sitting beside me noticed my book. "Oh, my God, I love that movie," he exclaimed. "I've watched it, like, thirty times!" He then went on to tell me that back in college, he and his friends had what they'd called "The Lebowski Challenge." Participants would watch the movie and every time a character drank a white Russian, they had to down one, and every time a time a character smoked a joint, they also had to light up. "Nobody ever made it through," my fellow traveler admitted. Before the final credits rolled, all participants had either passed out or puked. Or both.

From my point of view, any film that could have inspired this drinking/drugging game is an unlikely candidate to be a Buddhist cinematic classic. Nonetheless, in certain circles *The Big Lebowski* is celebrated for its dharmic wisdom. Maybe this shouldn't strike me as strange. While puritans like me abound, Buddhist history is peppered with practitioners on the wild side. In the Tibetan tradition, there is the mishap lineage that Jeff Bridges is so fascinated by, and in the Zen world there are such iconoclastic figures as the monk Ikkyu, who not only drank heavily but also apparently visited brothels wearing his robes because he believed sexual intercourse was a religious rite.

Bridges was skeptical when Glassman first told him that many people consider the Dude to be a Zen master. During the making of the film, no one claimed any such thing – neither the actors nor the film's creators, the renowned Coen brothers, Joel and Ethan.

Glassman laughed. "Just look at their name – the Koan brothers." He went on to assert that *The Big Lebowski* is filled with modern-day koans: "The Dude abides – very Zen, man. Or the Dude is not in – classic Zen."

According to Merriam-Webster, to abide means to wait, to endure without yielding, to bear patiently, to accept without objection. "That is no easy feat, especially in a culture that is success-driven, instant-gratification-oriented, and impatient, like ours," Bridges says in *The Dude and the Zen Master*. "True abiding is a spiritual gift that requires great mastery. The moral of the story, for me, is: be kind."

Yet the Dude isn't some idealized bodhisattva. As Glassman points out, he's "a lot like us. Stuff upsets him, like when someone pees on his rug. He has thoughts, frustrations, and everything that we all have, but he doesn't work from them. He works from where he is."

That is, the Dude is authentic. When he gets bent out of shape, he doesn't feign tranquility but quickly readjusts to his new circumstances, showing that he isn't attached to a self-image or identity. "Since he abides nowhere," continues Glassman, "he is free to abide everywhere."

In stark contrast is Walter, the Dude's bowling buddy played by John Goodman. Walter suffers intensely because he can't accept that in life there are strikes and gutters, ups and downs. In Walter's own words, "This won't stand, man." He's attached to his opinions and, because his opinions are so odd, so extreme, and so blatantly untrue, he helps us see the holes in all opinions, even our own. Even when we think our opinions are sacred.

"A lot of people say that my boss, this guy Shakyamuni Buddha, talked about the four noble truths," Glassman ribs. "But what he really taught was 'the four noble opinions.'" We can't say that Buddhism is about not being attached to any truth, and then say there are four noble big ones. "There's a little contradiction there," says Glassman.

He then claims that, in constantly telling Donny to "Shut the fuck up," Walter is employing a standard Zen technique for relaxing opinions. It's in the same spirit as the Zen teacher Ummon striking his student Tozan for saying innocuous things, as recorded in the classic koan Tozan's Sixty Blows. Zen masters of this rough ilk, says Glassman, are "trying to get you to realize that what you're saying ain't the truth. It ain't the whole thing." In fact, "There ain't no whole thing. You've got to just be open."

Or as the Dude says, "That's just like your opinion, man."

So now for my opinion about *The Big Lebowski* and its dharmic thread. As I see it, the Dude indeed abides in a way that smells faintly of spirituality. Though I detect attachment to a certain sweet, milky cocktail, he's essentially unattached to material goods. If his dumpy apartment doesn't tip you off to this, you can see it in the understated way he describes losing a million dollars: "Lost a little money today."

By and large the Dude is also compassionate, thinking as he does about the safety of Bunny. But he's clearly fast and loose with the precepts. Beyond the aforementioned cocktails, he's not above a lie or two – if it means getting his soiled rug replaced. Moreover, he doesn't really practice the Zen ideal of effortless effort. Unemployed and smoking up in his bathtub while listening to whale music, the Dude is simply effortless. Right from the beginning, the Stranger who bookends the film tells it to us straight: the Dude "is a lazy man … quite possibly the laziest in Los Angeles county, which would place him high in the runnin' for the laziest worldwide." Don't think, though, that I don't have a soft spot for the Dude and his easygoing ways. It's just that, instead of lumping him into the Buddhist tradition, I think he merits his own, all-American religion. And, indeed, he has inspired one. It's called Dudeism and, if Dudeism.com is to be taken seriously, it boasts over 150,000 ordained priests worldwide. The home page offers this invitation: "Come join the slowest-growing religion in the world … an ancient philosophy that preaches non-preachiness, practices as little as possible, and above all, uh … lost my train of thought there."

The Hebrew word for peace is *shalom*, and to Roshi Bernie Glassman it's the key to his work with the Zen Peacemakers. It's a word many people are familiar with, but what's less commonly known is that the root of shalom is *shalem*, meaning whole. Therefore, to make peace is to make whole, and in Zen – according to Glassman – the practice is to realize the wholeness and interconnectedness of life.

Glassman had a profound experience of wholeness in the early '70s, shortly after finishing his mathematics Ph.D. He was driving to work one morning when he had a vision of hungry ghosts everywhere. Called *pretas* in Buddhist cosmology, these are beings who experience (and represent) endless and unfulfillable desire. At first, he saw these hankering, unsatisfied beings as existing outside himself. But suddenly he had the keen sense that there was no separation: he was those beings, they were him. Glassman knew then that his life's calling was to feed the hungry, literally and figuratively. He would not stay forever holed up in a zendo but would take the realizations won on the cushion out into the world.

In 1982, Glassman and his students opened the Greyston Bakery in Yonkers, New York, a city plagued by unemployment, violence, and drugs. His vision was that a business could have a double bottom line; it could both generate profits and serve the community. On the ground this meant hiring people who would conventionally be considered unemployable. But – contrary to what some might expect – this was no recipe for disaster. In fact, Greyston was soon baking cakes and tarts for some of the most exclusive eateries in New York and making brownies for Ben & Jerry's ice cream. Today, the bakery is a solid $6 million business with over 75 employees.

And it's just one piece of a larger socially responsible business model. What has become known as the Greyston Foundation also includes the Greyston Family Inn, the Maitri Center, and Issan House. The Greyston Family Inn offers hundreds of low-cost permanent apartments for homeless families and a child-care center, after-school programs, and tenant-support services. Maitri is a medical center that serves people with AIDS-related illnesses, and Issan House provides housing for many of Maitri's patients.

In 1994, on Glassman's fifty-fifth birthday, he decided to establish the Zen Peacemakers Order. Originally, it was intended strictly for Zen practitioners, but it eventually blossomed into an international, interfaith network. As articulated by Glassman, the community is founded on three tenets for integrating spiritual practice and social action: (1) not-knowing, thereby giving up fixed ideas about ourselves and the universe, (2) bearing witness to the joy and suffering of the world, and (3) loving action for ourselves and others.

Glassman sees these three tenets as the essence of Zen, phrased in a fresh, modern idiom. "In Zen training," says Glassman, "koan study gets you to experience the state of not knowing." Then bearing witness is just sitting, or shikantaza, and loving action is none other than compassion.

In terms of peace and justice work, Glassman explains the three tenets by saying that positive change doesn't come out of an activist having fixed ideas. What really helps is being completely open and listening deeply. "I try to become the situation," he says, "and then I let the actions come out of that."

Bearing witness is at the heart of the groundbreaking retreats for which Glassman has become best known: street retreats and retreats held at the concentration camps of Auschwitz-Birkenau. Street retreats combine meditation with living as a homeless person for several days, with no money, no shelter, no job, no usual identity. Retreatants take their meals in soup kitchens and learn to survive without even the guarantee of a bathroom. Roshi Pat Enkyo O'Hara, a Buddhist teacher who was given dharma transmission by Glassman, has said that the power of a street retreat lies in how it pushes things "right in your face ... so there is no way to exclude anything. Living on the street is scary. But the minute you include the fear in your practice, it's much less scary because then the fear is there. You can touch it, you can feel it, and it's not this black cloud that's following you around."

During the bearing-witness retreats at Auschwitz-Birkenau, the lion's share of each day is spent sitting by the infamous train tracks, alternating silence with chanting the names of the victims. Glassman was originally inspired to hold these retreats when he went to Auschwitz for an interfaith conference.

"I walked into Birkenau," he told me, and "I could feel the millions of souls crying out to be remembered. I said I have got to bear witness to what's going on here. I spent a year and a half creating a format, which involved bringing together people from all walks of life – children and grandchildren of SS members, survivors, children of survivors, people from many countries, many religions." The first Auschwitz bearing witness retreat was held in 1996 and subsequent retreats have been held there every year since.

Their mutual commitment to social action is a big connection between Bernie Glassman and Jeff Bridges. Stamping out hunger is Bridges' main focus, and he has been dedicated to it for almost as long as he's been in film. A cofounder of the End

Hunger network, he is also the national spokesman for Share Our Strength's No Kid Hungry campaign; in the capacity of this role, he was recently invited to speak to both Republican and Democratic governors.

You might think that such a speech would be no big deal for an actor, but Bridges tied himself up in knots over it. It was four pages long, and he painstakingly memorized every word of it as though it were a monologue. Yet he was keenly aware that a speech is not a movie. There would not be take after take until he got it right – this was a one-shot deal, and the stakes were high. It was imperative that he impress upon both Republican and Democratic governors that childhood hunger is an issue that should transcend the political divide.

As it turned out, nothing was what Bridges expected. The first surprise was that his speech to the Republican governors was scheduled for the peculiar hour of 10:30 p.m. The second surprise was that he would have to compete with booze and bowling pins; that is, his speech was to be delivered first in a bar and then repeated a little later in a bowling alley. To make matters worse, the 10:30 speech got postponed to eleven, then midnight, and finally it got rolled into the one at the bowling alley.

"Virginia Governor Bob McDonnell, who is chairman of the Republican Governors Association and already part of the No Kid Hungry campaign, arrives, gives me a wonderful introduction, and splits," Bridges recounts in *The Dude and the Zen Master*. "It turns out that there are no other governors there at all. I end up giving the talk I'd agonized over for two months to an audience of seventy-five college girls at the bowling-alley bar. And I don't change a thing, either. I memorized my lines so well that I just give the entire four-page speech written for state governors – *I hope you'll join Governor McDonnell and others to develop state solutions to childhood hunger* – to a bunch of college girls."

Not that Bridges is putting these young women down. He's quick to add that – you never know – one fine day it just might be one of those girls who really makes a difference.

At the Four Seasons lounge, Bernie Glassman clarifies that the koans in *The Big Lebowski* are "not from Jeff," but rather from the Coen Brothers' script. "Jeff just happens to be the guy who is the Dude in the movie, and he's also the Dude in his life." I think Glassman means that, although Bridges isn't exactly the Dude you see in the film, he isn't exactly not that Dude either. The ways in which he is un-Dude are easy to pinpoint. Bridges, for instance, is no perennial bachelor. He's been married to the same woman for thirty-five years and they have three grown daughters. Nonetheless, Bridges has a duderino flavor – he's chilled out and, for lack of a better word, really nice. Frequently when someone asks him for an autograph, he goes five steps further and offers them a drawing instead. Also like the Dude, Bridges' speech is garnished with f-bombs and *mans*, but maybe he and Glassman are just hamming it up for the press. Bridges' tuna tartare is gone and Glassman's Danish is slightly picked over when the publicist approaches the table. It seems that Bridges' makeup artist and the rest of the bromantic couple's entourage are already anticipating the next media event, this one on TV. "Five more minutes," says the publicist.

Bridges screws up his face. "Cool, cool, yeah," he says, "but we were just getting going here!"

Pure Fiction

Susan Dunlap, Cary Groner, and Kim Stanley Robinson – Three Buddhist-Inspired Novelists

W hen I was first introduced to Darcy Lott, she was at work as a stunt double, wearing what she dubbed "the world's shortest kimono" and preparing to hurl herself off the turret of a Victorian building. She was careful while preparing for the stunt – or wanted to believe she was – but she got distracted at the last minute when a spotlight panned the dark street and she saw her long-lost brother, or what looked like him, on the roof of the Barbary Coast Zen Center. Suddenly the camera was on Darcy and she had to jump. No time to recheck her stunt prep, she missed the catcher bag and crashed into the sidewalk, injuring her shoulder. Was it a coincidence that the very next day an old friend of Darcy's disappeared, echoing the painful disappearance of her brother twenty years earlier?

This is the beginning of *Hungry Ghosts*, Susan Dunlap's second book in her Darcy Lott mystery series. But now, with the release of *No Footprints* this August, Dunlap is up to number five. She's also the author of three other mystery series, one suspense novel, and a collection of short stories, bringing her total number of published books to twenty-four. Of her books, the Darcy Lott series is most clearly about Buddhism. Yet, according to Dunlap, all of them have a Buddhist element. "They do, because I do," she says.

Buddhist fiction is a slippery fish to define. Some would say it's comprised solely of stories written by Buddhists and/or stories that feature Buddhist characters. Others would expand the definition to include stories written by non–Buddhist authors about non–Buddhist characters, as long as the writing reflects a Buddhist sensibility in addressing themes such as suffering, compassion, and emptiness. The Buddhist canon becomes very large indeed, however, if we go with the more liberal definition. Novelists – Buddhist and otherwise – are interested in the human condition. And since Buddhism rests on a foundation of universal human truths, it's common for writers of all faiths and traditions to express some Buddhist ideas in their work, even if they are unschooled in Buddhism. As Charles Johnson wrote in his foreword to *Nixon Under the Bodhi Tree and Other Works of Buddhist Fiction*, "The Buddhist experience is simply the *human* experience." Nonetheless, novelists who have studied or practiced Buddhism tend to offer a refreshing perspective by consciously weaving the dharma into their stories.

You could call fiction a lie. It's an invention, a fantasy. But fiction writers are using their "lies" to tell the truth – as they see it – about our world. And in showing us their truth, they offer us a path to compassion. Novels, written well, take us directly into the hearts and minds of others. These others may be fictional characters but they're also a lot like our friends and families, our enemies and adversaries, and the strangers on the subway or at the grocery store. When we read novels, we see why characters are driven to do what they do, and by extension we get a glimpse of the inner lives of the real people who are all around us.

In her life, Susan Dunlap has been immediately sure of three things: Zen, her husband, and the city of Berkeley. In the 1970s she walked into a zendo for the first time and felt instantly at home. An only child, she'd been raised by parents of different religions – one Catholic, one Protestant – and whatever conflict there'd been in the family was over that difference. As a result, she learned that spirituality was an important issue and that she could make her own decision about it.

According to Dunlap, Zen is a fit for her because it doesn't demand that practitioners accept doctrine per se; instead it emphasizes practitioners' own experience. She says, "I want to be able to sit quietly facing the wall and know that what is real is what's going on in this moment, and that there's nothing else forced upon me."

It was Dunlap's husband who got her interested in Eastern spirituality when he gave her a copy of *Autobiography of a Yogi*. They met in 1968 and, as she puts it, they've been married "forever." Her theory is that when your job is writing the thrilling stuff of murder mysteries, you don't need constant change and excitement in your relationships. Laughing, she adds, "When you kill people in fiction, you don't need to kill them in your regular life."

It was early on in her marriage when Dunlap began writing mysteries. One day she was reading an Agatha Christie novel, and she turned to her husband and said, "You know, I could do this." There was sort of a long pause from him, as if he were holding back a rude comment. Then he said, "Well, go ahead."

She did, but it wasn't quite as easy as she'd thought. Her first novel, which was about twins and encounter groups, didn't get picked up by a publisher. Nor did her second novel, her third, her fourth, her fifth… but she kept pounding away at her typewriter because she loved writing. Finally, on her seventh book, she landed a publisher.

Book by book, a pattern has emerged that place plays a central role in Dunlap's writing. This reflects the role of place in her life. She grew up in and around New York City. Then in 1968 she met someone who told her it was always warm and sunny in California. It had been zero degrees for a month in New York and there was a garbage strike raging. Dunlap packed her bags and headed west.

With only one exception, all of Dunlap's books are set in California and, while Berkeley is her first love, the whole San Francisco Bay Area has inspired her work. *No Footprints*, for example, revolves around a mysterious woman who attempts to jump off the Golden Gate Bridge. When the protagonist Darcy Lott prevents the suicide, the woman disappears into the night with the words: "By the weekend, I'll be dead."

Buddhism and mysteries make a good pairing, says Dunlap, because both ask you "to dismiss what is inessential. To look at what is. In a mystery, things are not as they seem, so what the detective is trying to do is see what the real facts are as opposed to all the things that cover up those facts. That is, the things that other people intend to make the detective believe, the things that the detective herself assumes."

Mysteries are also a succinct reflection of the Buddhist concept of karma. As Dunlap explains it, at the heart of every murder mystery is a dead person. In normal life, people are killed all the time and they don't necessarily bring their fate upon themselves. But in a mystery – for it to work – they do in some fashion have to draw the murderer to them. Otherwise, readers won't really care about the story. The victim in a mystery can cause their murder by doing something evil or conniving or by doing something innocent or even well intentioned. "The important thing," says Dunlap, "is that they have done something to set in motion the wheel of karma in their lives."

* * *

Cary Groner discovered Buddhism in high school and immediately resonated with it. But his mother thought meditation was peculiar and forbade him to do it. "I'd get caught meditating the way that other kids get caught smoking dope or shoplifting," says Groner, the author of *Exiles*. "Fortunately, meditation is something you can do without making any noise or attracting any attention, so at night I'd sneak out of bed and sit on the floor and practice." It felt quite subversive, which made it all the more appealing.

In his twenties, Groner felt the need for a Buddhist teacher and searched for a fit. Then one day in 1985 he was in Powell's Bookstore in Portland when he saw a poster for a talk by Chagdud Tulku Rinpoche. "In the poster Rinpoche was laughing and had this look that was fierce and funny and profound all at once," says Groner. "I remember thinking this might be the guy."

And he was.

Groner spent the next couple of years living at Chagdud Tulku's center in Cottage Grove, Oregon. "Rinpoche was the full package," says Groner. "He had deep insight and compassion, yet he was also totally down to earth and very funny. That's not to say the relationship was all peaches and cream. He had quite a temper and could get wrathful. Being with him was by turns exalting and terrifying but Rinpoche hammered away at the encrustation of habits I came in with and I did my best to hang in with that process."

These days, Groner is studying with Chagdud Tulku's lineage holder, Lama Drimed Norbu. He does a retreat every summer and he's part of a small group in the Bay Area that meets to do *tsok*, a Vajrayana Buddhist practice of offering and purification. From Groner's point of view, he's lucky. As a writer working from home, he can usually sit for a couple of hours each morning.

Groner writes in various genres. He has more than twenty years of journalism under his belt and writes often about health care, specializing in lower extremity biomechanics. He's been writing plays and poetry since he was a teenager and fiction since his twenties. That said, years went by without him having much success with creative writing. "I wrote plays and couldn't get them produced," he tells me. "I wrote screenplays and couldn't sell them and I wrote a couple of really terrible novels. Finally, I decided if I was going to do this I had to stop screwing around and really bring some commitment to it."

In 2006, Groner began his MFA in fiction writing at the University of Arizona, and his thesis eventually became *Exiles*, for which he landed a book deal with Spiegel & Grau, an imprint of Random House. *Exiles* is the story of cardiologist Peter Scanlon, who takes a look at the rubble of his failed marriage and moves to Kathmandu to volunteer at a health clinic. Never imagining the risks and hardships he'd find there, Peter takes his seventeen-year-old daughter with him. The poverty, the child prostitution, the shortage of medical supplies, and the unfamiliar diseases are all a shock, but the encroaching civil war could cost father and daughter their very lives.

"When I started writing *Exiles*, I was interested in the overlap between Buddhist thought and the sciences," says Groner. "So, my idea was to write an epistolary novel, an exchange of letters between a Tibetan lama and an evolutionary biologist. But it didn't take long to realize that would be interesting to me and about five other people on earth. If I wanted anyone to actually read the thing, I had to come up with a narrative."

Out of this realization, Groner eventually developed a fast-paced plot, honed draft by draft. There are keys to creating suspense, he learned. Within the overarching conflicts that form the narrative's spine, there need to be other problems that twist and turn, so that every time a character solves one problem it creates another. That way, there's always a challenge that characters are working on. "This is very much like life," says Groner, "like samsara."

The action-packed storyline may have been a departure from Groner's original idea for *Exiles*, but one element, at least, has remained the same: the theme of science meeting Buddhism. In the finished book, the science angle manifests as Peter, the American doctor with his background in biology, while the Buddhist angle manifests as a Tibetan lama. Peter and the lama meet in Nepal and their conversations challenge Peter to think deeply about issues such as evolution, the mind, and the nature of existence.

"Writing from a spiritual perspective can be tricky," says Groner. "You want to be true to your interests and experiences, but you never want to turn your work into propaganda. It's important to remember that your job is to write, not proselytize." Although *Exiles* deals with Buddhism, Groner is primarily focused on telling human stories and revealing how people are led by their foibles to some sort of crisis and then to understanding. "This," he says, "is what all storytellers do, regardless of whether they have spiritual inclinations or not."

Groner occasionally experiments with magical realism, but these days he does so sparingly. Despite his admiration for writers such as Gabriel García Márquez, Groner feels that, as a reader, unearthly happenings engage his skepticism and pull him out of a narrative. Magical realism, Groner says, can "distance the reader from the real human experience unfolding on the page."

"Real" is not a word that Groner hesitates to use when describing fiction, because, for him, fiction requires relentless honesty. As he puts it: "The revision process not only involves looking at structural issues, such as information release, rhythm, and tone. It also involves relentlessly ferreting out anything dishonest in the writing, by which I mean anything that is not how things are in real life."

Groner often hears writers claim that writing is their meditation. But in his opinion these two activities are distinct. Writing, for him, is more like a waking dream – the writer is following the story that he or she is creating. Meditation, on the other hand, is much more open and free. Yet Groner says there is one way writing and meditation are the same, and that's the flow they share, the way they both make you lose track of time.

"Writing and meditation are compatible," says Groner. "Anyone who's tried to sit quietly for periods of time knows the fantastical capabilities that get unleashed when all you're looking for is quiet. I sometimes keep a little pad and pen with me so that if I get a good idea I can jot it down and forget about it, because otherwise I try to hang onto it and it becomes extremely distracting.

"Sitting practice relaxes and opens my mind, and this allows for a kind of free play of the imagination that can be conducive to writing."

* * *

"Literature is my religion," says Kim Stanley Robinson. "The novel is my way of making sense of things." He doesn't meditate, nor does he call himself a Buddhist. Nonetheless, he's quick to acknowledge that Buddhism has had a profound impact on him and his writing. Zen philosophy, in particular, has taught him to stay in the moment, to pay attention to the natural world, and to ground himself in work. In interviews he frequently speaks of the Zen rubric "chop wood, carry water," and claims that it could just as easily be "run five miles, write five pages." In Zen, according to Robinson, there is ritual in daily activities – gardening, washing dishes, looking after little children. "This puts a spark into things, a glow around them," he tells me. "It gives a meaning to life that I appreciate very much."

Robinson is best known for his science fiction trilogy about terraforming Mars – *Red Mars*, *Green Mars*, and *Blue Mars*. Buddhism does not play an obvious role in these titles. It does, however, in his alternative history novel *The Years of Rice and Salt* and in his series about climate change, which kicks off with *Forty Signs of Rain*. *The Years of Rice and Salt* is a re-imagining of the Black Death and its aftermath. According to history, the plague wiped out a third of Europe's population; then Europe recovered from the loss and colonized large pockets of the globe. But what if the plague had wiped out 99 percent of all Europeans instead? Perhaps, Robinson posits, Buddhism and Islam would have become the two most influential world religions. *The Years of Rice and Salt* is the tale of several main characters and their reincarnations, spanning the fourteenth century to the modern age. Over their lifetimes, the characters struggle to better themselves, and between lifetimes they meet in the *bardo*, the gap between death and rebirth according to the Tibetan Buddhist understanding.

Like Cary Groner, Kim Stanley Robinson is deeply interested in how Buddhism and science intersect and this is the theme he explores in *Forty Signs of Rain*. The book opens with the scientist Anna Quibler showing up for work one day at the

National Science Foundation and discovering that Khembalung, a country she's never heard of before, has established an embassy in the building. It turns out that Khembalung is a small, new country of exiled Tibetan Buddhists, who originally hail from the mythical kingdom of Shambhala, and that among the monks at the embassy is the Panchen Lama. That is, Robinson clarifies, "the real Panchen Lama who the Dalai Lama designated, who the Chinese immediately kidnapped, and who has been disappeared ever since. Well, in my novel he's living under a pseudonym in the NSF building."

Forty Signs of Rain was inspired in part by the Dalai Lama, particularly his thoughts on the common ground shared by science and Buddhism. Scientists and Buddhists both investigate the nature of reality; they both look at the world and ask, How can we make things better? How can we reduce suffering?

"I could not be more impressed by the current Dalai Lama," says Robinson. "He's always a presence in my house – his photo is on the refrigerator and next to my desk." When Robinson read that the Dalai Lama was going to speak in Washington D.C., he got tickets and flew out. "It was bizarre," says Robinson. "There I was at the Washington Wizards basketball arena with 13,000 people, and the Dalai Lama was speaking. I put this event straight into the novel exactly as it happened. I couldn't help it – it was so incredible."

These days, Robinson writes his novels outdoors in a little courtyard on the north side of his house. It's shady there, so he can see his laptop screen, and he simply puts a tarp overhead if it's raining and bundles up if it's cold. As he puts it, being outdoors transforms writing into an adventure, into an interaction with about fifty little birds, the trees, the clouds, the changing of the seasons.

Nature and ecology have always played a significant role in Robinson's life. When he was a child, the coastal plain of Southern California was orchard country, planted with lemon and orange groves, avocado and eucalyptus. At age ten, Robinson believed he was the Huck Finn of this terrain and he dressed like him, exploring the irrigation ditches and the creeks. But in his teenage years, the bucolic orchards were ripped up and replaced with the concrete of condominiums and freeways. This made science fiction feel eerily familiar when he started reading it. In the rapid change and heavy-duty mechanization of the fictional future worlds, he recognized his own home. "It struck me," says Robinson, "that science fiction was my realism."

In his SF, Robinson strives to convey a sense of hope about the environment, because he feels that despite the bad choices we're making right now, we're not necessarily creating a dystopia or apocalypse. "Science is powerful, people are smart, and there's potential to have both good and bad at once," he says. But people need to think deeply about possible ecological solutions, and fiction can be an accessible foundation for doing so. "I want to leave people with the sense of having had a lot of fun reading a novel, but I also want to lead them to interesting questions. That's really what science fiction always does."

In addition to SF, Robinson also resonates with poetry, and when the renowned Beat poet Gary Snyder was teaching at U.C. Davis, he informally audited classes with him. "I was writing my novels at the same time," says Robinson, "so taking a break for Gary's class put extra stress on my novel writing schedule. But it was worth it because Gary is truly an exemplary figure. I always joke that Zen Buddhism must be good for you – Gary is living proof of it. And he jokes himself about how, after spending ten years sitting on his butt, everything looks good to him ever afterwards. But he's a very positive force in a lot of people's lives, including mine. He's informal, but very sharp, very generous. I think he always thought I was an oddball. You know, what is this science fiction author doing in my class writing second-rate nature poetry?"

Then Snyder's late wife convinced Snyder to try Robinson's *Red Mars* and he crunched through the whole trilogy, saying he never knew science fiction could be that good. Snyder is now retired but the two writers have become friends and they see each other whenever Snyder visits Davis.

According to Robinson, writing is intimately connected to impermanence, to the fleeting present moment. "We're always in the present," he says. "There's a present in which I write sentences. Then later there's a present in which someone else looks at those sentences – the black marks on the page – and at that moment in their mind they make up a story based on the sentences that they read, as well as images from their own life. So, there are the black marks on the paper, which are always there and continue year after year to be the same, but the book is only alive when someone's reading it. It's an interesting kind of impermanence. It's similar to music in that you always have the scores but you don't have the performances except when it's being played."

Reading, concludes Robinson, is what makes fiction live.

The Buddha Was Here

On Pilgrimage in India

The National Museum in New Delhi doesn't usually welcome visitors until 10 a.m., but on the first morning of the
2018 International Buddhist Conclave, they open their doors
early for us. This, the sixth edition of the conclave, is attended
by nearly three hundred people from twenty-nine countries. We
are journalists and monastics, travel agents and scholars. We are
Buddhists from many traditions and non-Buddhists. Our purpose
is to connect with each other and explore the potential of Buddhist pilgrimage in India.

As I'm filing through security, I have no idea what treasures
the National Museum houses. So as far as I know, this museum
visit doesn't have a direct connection to the conclave's mission.
It's just a nice add-on for those of us who are interested. And I
am interested – in everything. This is my first time in India, a
place I have always longed to visit.

I marvel at an elegant bronze figurine of a dancer from the
Indus Valley, circa 2500 BCE. I laugh when Shantum Seth, an
Indian dharma teacher in Thich Nhat Hanh's Plum Village tradition, quips that the ancient dinnerware on display looks as if
it could have come from Ikea. (He's right!) But most memorable
of all, I feel a quiet thrill when I come to the Buddhist artifacts
and, though I'm being hurried along, I pause for as long as I can
in front of a depiction of the Buddha's birth. As was the artistic
custom in the early centuries of Buddhism, the Buddha himself
is not shown – just a symbol to represent him, his footprints.

Along with the other delegates, I'm ushered into a room
that's been prepared for us for meditation and I quietly take a seat
on the floor. We sit facing an intricate pavilion, gleaming with
gold, that was crafted from teak by Thai artists. This pavilion is

roped off and behind glass, and I don't know what it holds until someone whispers in my ear: they're bone fragments from the Buddha.

But are they really? The Buddha died so long ago. How can we know that these bits of skull belonged to him and not to someone else? This is a valid question. Yet as Shantum Seth rings the bell and a clutch of Theravadin monks in saffron robes begins to drone their Pali chants, it's not a question that concerns me. What's touching me is the fact that the Buddha had bones – and flesh – at all.

So often we talk about the Buddha as if he were a figure from mythology, not a human being like you and me. Generation after generation, for thousands of years, we've revered his wisdom so much that in our imagination he has become more of a deity than a person, and his life story has been embellished with fantastical flourishes – the stuff of legends. Maybe it's because we want there to be someone who is more than human to save us. Maybe it's because it's so hard to grasp a time like 500 BCE, which is around when the Buddha lived. It sounds so far in the past that maybe it was never.

But now I'm meditating in front of ancient bone and, for a moment, it feels as if the Buddha has reached through the centuries and tapped me on the shoulder. *I was real,* he seems to say. *I was here.*

This is how the story goes. Twenty-six centuries ago, in the foothills of the Himalayas, Queen Mahamaya dreamed of a white elephant with a lotus in its trunk. The elephant circled her three times and then entered her womb. Since elephants were considered a symbol of greatness, this dream was taken as a sign that Mahamaya would have an extraordinary child.

In those days it was customary for a woman to return to her parents' house to give birth. So, when Mahamaya felt the time had come, she set out for her ancestral home. Along the way she stopped in Lumbini, a garden in what is now Nepal, and there she delivered her child. It is said that heavenly beings showered down flower petals and the newborn – shining like the sun – took seven paces in each direction and wherever he stepped, a lotus sprang up.

It was prophesied that the boy, named Siddhartha, would grow up to become either a great king or a great spiritual leader. His father – hoping that Siddhartha would dedicate himself to the political realm – tried to guide him in that direction by sheltering Siddhartha within the luxurious confines of his palaces. When Siddhartha was sixteen years old, he married Yasodhara, who was also of his clan, and the couple eventually had a son.

But then, at age twenty-nine, Siddhartha got a glimpse of the troubled world his father had protected him from. Out driving with his charioteer, he saw – for the very first time – old age, disease, and death, and he learned that this degeneration was the inescapable human condition. The prince was shocked. How could everyone just go about their lives, seeking silly pleasures, as if this shadow weren't hanging over them?

While mired in this thought, Siddhartha saw a holy man. Dressed simply, this man had such a peaceful look on his face that Siddhartha knew what he needed to do. In the middle of the night he slipped away, leaving his family and royal life behind. This is how he took his first step on the spiritual path.

Siddhartha found a holy man and mastered his teachings; then he found another and mastered his. Yet Siddhartha still felt that something was missing in his understanding, so following the suggestion of the great Jain teacher Mahavira, he dedicated himself to asceticism. Siddhartha's approach was extreme and left him skeletal and weak. Rigidly practicing meditation, he held his breath for long, dangerous periods of time and ate only what would fit in the hollow of his palm.

Eventually, Siddhartha finally realized that this self-mortification was going to kill him, not lead him to enlightenment. What he actually needed to advance spiritually was a middle way, neither worldly indulgence nor harsh austerities. On Siddhartha's thirty-fifth birthday, he broke his fast when a young village woman named Sujata made him an offering: a bowl of sweetened rice cooked in milk.

Sujata's gift gave Siddhartha the strength to cross the Nairanjana River, and on the other side, on a sandy bank, he came to a large tree with heart-shaped leaves. Siddhartha sat beneath it and, in full lotus facing east, vowed that he would stay there until he reached enlightenment. This type of tree became known as a *ficus religiosa* – a Bodhi tree.

Since I was a kid, I've always thought of large trees as generous, stable grandfathers, quietly offering shade and support. But the tree the Buddha sat under was more like an old teacher – kind and venerable. I imagine Siddhartha contemplating the heart-shaped leaves and seeing in them the sunshine and rain, the earth and clouds, and in that way, I imagine the tree teaching him dependent arising: *if this exists, that exists; if this ceases to exist, that also ceases to exist.*

Though the original Bodhi tree is long gone, its place has been taken by what's believed to be a direct descendent. In the Buddha's time, the tree was rooted in a rural setting, but over the centuries a town by the name of Bodhgaya has grown up around it. Bodhgaya is located in the modern Indian state of Bihar – the poorest in India – and the nearest airport is in Gaya, intense and busy like all Indian cities.

I arrive on a chartered flight with the other delegates of the International Buddhist Conclave, which is sponsored by the government of India. We're given an exuberant, flower-filled welcome and herded onto eight buses festooned with marigold garlands, long stemmed red roses, and ribbons. Driving to Bodhgaya, the buses stick together as if they are a train. A police escort leads us, and children wave as we pass by.

Finally, we get to the site of the Buddha's awakening, and there, silhouetted against the sky, is the Mahabodhi temple, a tall, graceful pyramid rising from a square platform. Everywhere I look people are meditating. They're monastic and lay; in robes and in jeans; doing traditional practice or their own thing. One man has his eyes covered and a bottle of water balanced in each hand, as if they were Chinese meditation balls. There's also the odd stray dog.

Bodhgaya is the most important pilgrimage site in the Buddhist world, and it's believed that even in the Buddha's time there was a shrine here. At first, the Bodhi tree was marked simply by a two-storey wooden structure and stone throne. Then in the third century, Ashoka, the Mauryan king who was instrumental in spreading Buddhism in India, ordered the construction of a commemorative temple. Mahabodhi was originally built in the sixth century and over the years has been destroyed and rebuilt several times.

Along with the rest of the delegates, I take my place under the Bodhi tree, which is right beside the temple. Sitting on oriental rugs that have been laid out for us, we face an altar laden with dragon fruit, pomegranates, pink roses, and a statue of the Buddha. A Theravadin monk lights a lamp, and the chanting begins, then builds, and finally stops. Slowly, I let go of my rushing and grasping and find my breath.

Shantum Seth, who sits facing me and the other delegates, rings a bell. "Our teacher, the Buddha, sat under the Bodhi tree for forty-nine days and nights and then continued to be with the Bodhi tree for another forty-nine days," he says. "So we look at the Bodhi tree as our spiritual ancestor and we sit with her in the same way the Buddha did – in the present moment."

Seth holds a yellow Bodhi leaf in his hand and glances down at it occasionally. Focusing on our breath, he continues, our body and mind come together. Often our body is here but our mind is elsewhere. Meditation trains the mind to come back to the present and gives us a way to look more deeply into what's going on both inside of us and outside.

Seth rings the bell again and guides us to straighten our backs, relax our shoulders, and feel the gentle rise and fall of our bellies. He has a soothing voice, which eventually dissolves into silence. Now, we are hundreds of people, all together, listening to nothing but our breathing and the chorus of birds calling from the branches above our heads.

Later, I talk about our experience under the Bodhi tree with one of the non-Buddhist delegates, a journalist from Poland. Something about it touched her so deeply, she says, that it brought tears to her eyes. It was like she could feel the collective energy of generation after generation of people coming to this spot and finding stillness and quiet. It didn't matter that she wasn't a Buddhist.

Shantum Seth, in addition to being a dharma teacher, is also a longtime leader of Buddhist pilgrimage tours. Under the Bodhi tree, he says, people often find they have a deep sense of concentration and gratitude. "There are magical memories you can have," he continues. "You're sitting there meditating and then maybe a leaf falls onto your lap. You can take that leaf with you to your meditation space back home and put it on your altar to be reminded of this beautiful space where the Buddha – and you – practiced."

Siddhartha took his seat under the Bodhi tree on a full moon just before the rainy season. As our train of buses pulls away from Bodhgaya, I understand a little more about what it must have been like for him. We were also there when the moon was a perfect circle. While I was sitting under the Bodhi tree, a few cooling raindrops fell on my back. They felt like a gift.

After the Buddha achieved enlightenment, he pondered how he could share his realizations with others. The truth he had realized was difficult to grasp and ran hard against the grain of human desires. Most people, the Buddha knew, would turn away from his teachings, but he would try to teach those who could truly listen and understand.

The Buddha contemplated who he should teach first. He thought of the two holy men he'd studied with, but he knew they had passed away. Then he thought of the five men he'd practiced asceticism with. They'd shunned him when he started to practice the middle way, but he knew they were sincere seekers and might listen.

The five ascetics were residing in a park where deer roamed freely, in a place now called Sarnath, located in the Indian state of Uttar Pradesh. So, taking his leave of the Bodhi tree, the Buddha walked more than 160 miles to find his old companions. When they saw him coming, they resolved to ignore him, but there was something new and remarkable about his bearing and, despite themselves, they were drawn to him.

This, says Shantum Seth, is when "the Buddha became the buddhadharma." On that day in Deer Park, the Buddha taught for the very first time. In this, his first sermon, he taught the four noble truths, and in doing so laid the foundation of the world religion we know today as Buddhism. He taught the truths of suffering, the cause of suffering, the end of suffering, and the path.

An ascetic named Kaundinya was the first to realize the truth of the Buddha's teachings. Then soon after, the other four ascetics in the Deer Park came to the same realization. They were the first Buddhist monks, and the Buddhist sangha – the world's oldest continuous human institution – was born.

The Buddha went on to teach for forty-five years. He and his growing number of followers crisscrossed the plains of northern India, going everywhere on foot. He often returned to Sarnath and the surrounding area.

Today, the most iconic feature of Sarnath is the massive Dhamek Stupa, built in 500 CE. Stupas are Buddhist mound-like structures that often contain relics, but Dhamek is solid and relic-less. Other notable sites in this historic city include additional stupas and the Archaeological Museum Sarnath, which houses such antiquities as a lustrously polished sculpture of four lions, each facing a different direction. These four united felines were crafted under the auspices of King Ashoka and originally topped a pillar in Sarnath. Today they're recognized around the world as the official symbol of the Republic of India.

As I wander Sarnath, I linger near the Dhamek Stupa, feeling small next to its girth of more than ninety feet. From a distance, it looks unornamented but up close I can see that it's delicately chiseled with floral and geometric designs, human figures, and even geese. Geese, I'm told, symbolize the sangha because they're birds that live in community, taking turns leading and caring for each other. This reminds me of two Theravadin monastics – one elderly, one young – who are participating in the conclave. The young monk takes such tender care of his teacher.

Near the Dhamek Stupa stands the Mulagandhakuti Vihara, a temple established in 1931 with an interesting – and international – backstory. In 1891, Anagarika Dharmapala, a Buddhist revivalist from Ceylon, went on pilgrimage to India. At that time, the Mahabodhi Temple had recently been restored but – since Buddhism was no longer practiced in India – the temple had been converted into a place of worship of the Hindu deity Shiva.

When Dharmapala saw this, he resolved to help bring Buddhism back to India and, as part of his efforts, he spoke about Buddhism at the 1893 Parliament of the World's Religions in Chicago. On the way back, his ship docked in Hawaii and, there, Mary Foster, a friend of a friend, went to meet him. She was a wealthy American woman in emotional turmoil, and Dharmapala consoled her with Buddhist teachings. After that, Foster gave him a substantial donation, and he used that money to build Mulagandhakuti Vihara, marking where the Buddha meditated during his first rainy season retreat after awakening.

On the Mulagandhakuti grounds, there is a tree that, like the one in Bodhgaya, is said to be a descendent of the original Bodhi tree. Its spreading branches are said to symbolize the new growth of Buddhism in India. The temple exterior is embellished with spires, and the interior is graced by a golden statue of the Buddha and frescos depicting his life that were poignantly painted in soft hues by a Japanese artist. There, in front of me on the wall, is an image of the newly born Siddhartha taking his first steps. And there he is under the Bodhi tree, with Sujata presenting him with her food offering. Finally, there he is stretched out on his side in death – his final resting posture.

According to the *Mahaparinirvana Sutra*, the Buddha said it is of great benefit for practitioners to go on pilgrimage to the four places associated with the most pivotal moments in his life: his birth, his enlightenment, his first teaching, and his death. But bear in mind that the point of pilgrimage isn't just veneration. As Shantum Seth explains, it "teaches us a healthy disregard for comfort. It helps us look at our own mind in an unhabituated way, and teaches patience and humility. You get to know yourself better."

When we go to these Buddhist pilgrimage sites, we gain new insight into the Buddha's teachings because we have a deeper understanding of his life and circumstances. Despite all the cars, cellphones, and skyscrapers, you can still connect with the India the Buddha lived in 2,600 years ago. Village life is cut from same ancient cloth, and you can meet a modern-day Sujata, serving something sweet and energizing. The rivers and caves you read about in the sutras are still there, too. Farmers still plow their fields behind water buffalo the same way they did in the Buddha's time. On pilgrimage, says Seth, "The Buddha's story becomes real. You're seeing the whole context of his life. You're breathing the same air he did."

In the Mulagandhakuti temple, I take another long look at the fresco of the Buddha stretched out in death. He died from food poisoning in Kushinagar, in present-day Uttar Pradesh. He was in his eighties and, like every other human being, he'd experienced various mundane ailments his whole life. Sickness, age, fatigue, death – these are the realities of a human body, even the body of the Buddha.

Now, in this place where the Buddha is said to have spent a rainy season meditating, I feel as if he just whispered in my ear, then slipped out the temple door. He seemed to say to me that although he was not eternal, his teachings are, and the beautiful, inspiring thing about his being human is that it means there's hope for all of us. We – just like the Buddha – have the potential to awaken.

I stand in front of the golden Buddha at the altar and light a candle. Then, following my breath, I watch the flame dance and burn.

For Love of Nature

A Q&A with Jane Goodall

Wanting to know where eggs came from, the five-year-old Jane Goodall ensconced herself for hours in a henhouse, oblivious to the fact that her family was worriedly looking for her. But the little girl didn't get scolded when she got home. Her mother saw how excited she was, so she simply listened to the details of the discovery.

The years passed, and Goodall's passion and patience for observing wildlife only grew. In 1960, she began her study of chimpanzees and soon rocked the scientific community with what she learned: chimpanzees make and use tools. Prior to this, it was believed only humans had this skill. On hearing of Goodall's observation, the anthropologist and paleontologist Louis S.B. Leakey famously said: "Now we must redefine tool, redefine Man, or accept chimpanzees as humans." Goodall went on to make further groundbreaking discoveries that helped solidify the evolutionary link between chimpanzees and humans.

Today Goodall is seventy-nine and travels three hundred days a year in order to spread the word on environmental issues. I spoke to her via phone when she was spending a rare day at her home in the United Kingdom. She talked about the compassion of animals, the power of trees, and what we can all do to effect positive change in the world.

For decades, you've championed wildlife and the environment. How do you maintain hope?

My reason for hope is – first of all – my youth program, Roots and Shoots. This is the way I explain why it's called that: children are like plants. They start out as a tiny seed. Then wee roots and shoots appear. They're weak at first, but the power within the seed is so magical that the little roots reach water and the little shoots reach the sun. Eventually, they can push rocks aside and work through cracks in a brick wall. They can even knock a wall down. The rocks and the walls are the problems we've inflicted on the planet – environmental and social – but roots and shoots surround the world. Plants can change the world; they can undo a spot of the damage we've created. And young people are definitely going to change the world. As I travel around, I meet the youth. They're filled with hope and enthusiasm and innovative ideas, and that's very inspiring. Roots and Shoots is now in 132 countries.

Secondly, my reason for hope is the resilience of nature. The places that we've destroyed can become beautiful again. And then there's the human brain, which is utterly amazing. I think of the scientists who drilled down into the permafrost and brought up the remains of an Ice Age squirrel's nest. In the plant material, they found three living cells and from those living cells they managed to recreate the plant, which was a meadow's wheat. It's 32,000 years old, but it's now growing and seeding and reproducing. That's the resilience of nature, the incredible human brain, and the indomitable human spirit. Sometimes people say that something won't work, but there are other people – like the scientists who recreated this Ice Age plant – who don't give up. They overcome tremendous obstacles, and that's very inspiring. It gives me hope.

In your book, Seeds of Hope, you talk about the reverence people tend to feel when they're with trees. Why do you think trees engender these feelings?

They engender these feelings for me because – rooted in the ground – they can be so strong. They can withstand wind. They even withstand fire sometimes. It's difficult for me to stand by a tree with my hand on its bark and not feel that it has a spiritual value as well as a materialistic one. There is the whole symbolism of the roots going into the ground and finding water deep, deep down, and the leaves reaching up. There's the fact that they're purifying our air and removing the Co2.

You use the word spiritual. How would you define spirituality?

It's the opposite of being materialistic. Some people believe that everything is just there for its material value, or just as a thing. And then other people believe there's something more than that, which I happen to believe. I don't know if I can define spirituality – I'm not sure anybody really has – but it's something that you either feel or you don't. It's an awareness of life that's more than just the physical presence.

In your work as a primatologist and an ethologist, what anecdotal evidence have you discovered that demonstrates animals can feel compassion or love?

I'll give you one story. There was an infant chimpanzee named Mel. He was three and should still have been riding on his mother's back, sleeping with her at night, and suckling. but his mother died. If he'd had an older brother or sister, he would have been adopted by that individual, but he didn't, so he was on his own and we thought he'd die. Then he was adopted by Spindle, an unrelated male who was twelve, which is about like being a fifteen- or sixteen-year-old human. Spindle let little Mel ride on his back. If it was cold or Mel was frightened, he let him cling to his belly as a mother would. If Mel crept up to his nest at night and made whimpering sounds, Spindle reached out and drew him in. They slept curled up together. When Mel begged, whimpering with his hand out, Spindle would share his food. And most dramatic of all, Spindle protected Mel. Adolescent males tend to be scapegoats. If one male is being dominated by another, he takes it out on somebody lower ranking, so the adolescents keep out of the way in times of social excitement. And the mother's job is to keep her infant away, but of course, Little Mel didn't have a mother, so Spindle took that job on, even though it meant that he himself often got bashed by the adult male. There is no question that Spindle saved Mel's life.

What do you see as the most important thing individuals can do to effect positive change for the environment?

The most important thing we can do is remember that every single day every single one of us makes a difference. And we all can choose the kind of difference we're going to make. It does require becoming a little aware about what we buy. Where does it come from? How was it grown? Did it involve the use of child slave labor or chemical pesticides? And then there's all the little ways in which you interact with the environment. Do you bother to help a sick dog? Do you respond to appeals for help when somebody is in trouble?

The big problem today is that so many people feel insignificant. They feel that the problems facing the world are so huge that there's nothing they can do, so they do nothing. And as an individual maybe there really isn't that much, but when you get thousands, and then millions, of individuals all doing the best they can every day for the environment and for other beings, then you get huge change.

What are some concrete examples of taking small steps to effect change?

There's one man who moved to Japan, where he likes to walk in the woods. But sometimes there are violent storms and these little tiny tree orchids get blown down. Wanting to save them, he began taking the blown-down orchids home and looking after them. Now when the season is right, he gets as far up a tree as he can and staples them there with a stapler and they grow back. It's a simple thing, but it's rather charming.

Another example, I went into a radio station in Canada and in the studio waiting room I saw there were about six potted plants dotted around. They were all dying because they hadn't been watered. So I made a huge thing about it. Then when I went back a year later, all the plants were very healthy. So little things like that make a difference. Just never blame somebody. I mean, I didn't say to the people at the radio station, "Who's responsible for this monstrous behavior toward the plants?" I just said, "Oh, these poor little plants. Please can you find me some water? I want to look after them." It's all a question of how you go about trying to create change.

The Wanderer

A Profile of Mingyur Rinpoche

The old monk Lama Soto knocked on Yongey Mingyur Rinpoche's door. Then he knocked again. It was noon at Tergar Monastery in Bodhgaya, India, and Lama Soto was bringing Mingyur Rinpoche his lunch, just as he'd done for the past five days, ever since Mingyur Rinpoche had announced that he was going to intensify his practice and remain alone in his room, eating only once a day. Their custom was that Lama Soto would knock on the door; in response, Mingyur Rinpoche would open it a little, then Lama Soto would walk in. But on this day early last June, Mingyur Rinpoche did not open the door and no sound came from his room. At one o'clock, Lama Soto pushed open the unlocked door and, on the bed, he found a long white ceremonial scarf and a letter. Mingyur Rinpoche was gone and he had taken nothing with him – not money, not a change of clothes, not even a toothbrush. Lama Soto nearly fainted.

The letter, written in Tibetan, explained that from a young age Mingyur Rinpoche had wanted to practice by traveling alone from place to place in the style of a wandering yogi. Now he'd made the decision to do so. "Though I do not claim to be like the great masters of times past," he wrote, "I am now embarking on this journey as a mere reflection of these teachers, as a faithful imitation of the example they set. For a number of years, my training will consist of simply leaving behind my connections, so please do not be upset with my decision." He urged his students to continue practicing in his absence and not to worry about him.

More than eight months have passed since Mingyur Rinpoche disappeared, and still no one knows where he is. Cortland Dahl is the president of the board of Tergar International, a network of meditation centers and study groups under Mingyur

Rinpoche's guidance. When I ask Dahl if he has any guesses regarding his teacher's whereabouts, he tells me that the short answer is no, but that there have been rumors.

"I just heard on Facebook," Dahl tells me, "that he was seen at Tso Pema, which is a famous pilgrimage site in northern India, and I heard someone else say they had an unconfirmed sighting in Ladakh. I have no idea if they really did see him. But if anybody did, and he got the sense that people knew he was there, I'm sure the first thing he would do is pack up and head somewhere else."

Milarepa, whose life is the stuff of legends, is Tibet's most famous wandering yogi. About a thousand years ago, he was born into a prosperous family. But then his father died and Milarepa's aunt and uncle took control of the estate, forcing Milarepa and his sister and mother into servitude. This twisted Milarepa's mother into wanting revenge and she manipulated him into studying the black arts. Then one day, when his aunt and uncle were having a party to celebrate their son's engagement, Milarepa brewed up a storm that destroyed their house, killing thirty-five people. The villagers were furious and they set off to hunt him down, but Milarepa got word of their approach and conjured up a hailstorm. Later, however, the full force of his terrible deeds hit him and he was desolate with remorse.

It was at this point that Milarepa met Marpa, a powerful householder yogi, who recognized Milarepa as his future heart son, yet did not tell him. Instead, Marpa was hard on Milarepa. He yelled at him and hit him and refused to teach him at all until he'd built and demolished three stone towers, one after another. In this way, Marpa helped Milarepa to quickly burn away his negative karma, and then Milarepa was able to dedicate himself to Buddhist practice. Later, after he attained enlightenment, Milarepa assumed there was no longer any need for him to stay in the mountains and decided to go to cities and villages to teach people how to alleviate suffering. Before he could depart, however, he had a dream that Marpa told him to stay in retreat. If he did that, Marpa said, he would touch the lives of countless people through example.

Milarepa is remembered today for his beautiful, inspired songs and poetry. For half a lifetime, he wandered the mountains of Tibet. At one point, he lived in a cave and subsisted on nothing but nettle soup, leaving him bone thin and his skin a strange green. Frequently, people would discover that Milarepa, a realized master, was living nearby and they'd gather around him. When the crowds grew too thick, he'd move on.

Another well-known wandering yogi is Dza Patrul Rinpoche, a great Dzogchen master of the nineteenth century. Completely disinterested in fine clothes and titles, Patrul Rinpoche begged for his supper at nomad encampments. Sometimes it would come to pass that a great lama would arrive whom the nomads would greet with incense and prostrations. Then the lama would see Patrul Rinpoche and he'd hurl himself to the ground at Patrul Rinpoche's feet. Only in that way did the people understand the accomplishments of the threadbare wanderer.

Nyoshul Khen Rinpoche was one of the few recent adepts to practice as a wandering yogi. A Dzogchen master, he narrowly escaped Tibet in 1959 and then wandered the streets of Calcutta, begging and living among the Hindu sadhus. Khen Rinpoche, now deceased, was one of Mingyur Rinpoche's most influential teachers.

Yongey Mingyur Rinpoche was a rising star in the Buddhist world. The author of two bestselling books, he had a large community of students around the globe, and he was the abbot of Tergar Osel Ling Monastery in Nepal and Tergar Rigzin Khacho Targye Ling Monastery in India. Adding it all up, when he slipped away last June, he was leaving a lot behind.

Mingyur Rinpoche was born in Nubri, Nepal, in 1975 to an illustrious Tibetan family. His mother is Sönam Chödrön, a descendant of two Tibetan kings, and his father was the late Tulku

Urgyen Rinpoche, one of the most renowned Dzogchen teachers of the twentieth century. The couple's youngest son, Mingyur Rinpoche has three elder brothers who are themselves accomplished Buddhist teachers: Chokyi Nyima Rinpoche, Tsikey Chokling Rinpoche, and Tsoknyi Rinpoche.

Mingyur Rinpoche had what appeared on the surface to be idyllic early years. After all, he had a loving family and a home nestled in a beautiful Himalayan valley. But in *The Joy of Living* he makes a confession, one he acknowledges might sound strange coming from someone regarded as a reincarnate lama who supposedly did wonderful things in past lives. "From earliest childhood," Mingyur Rinpoche writes, "I was haunted by feelings of fear and anxiety. My heart raced and I often broke out in a sweat whenever I was around people I didn't know... Anxiety accompanied me like a shadow."

When Mingyur Rinpoche was about six years old, he found some relief meditating in the caves dotting the hills around his village. In these caves, generations of practitioners had meditated and in them Mingyur Rinpoche tried to follow in their footsteps by mentally chanting the mantra *Om Mani Padme Hum*. Though he didn't really understand what he was doing, this practice gave him a temporary calm. Nonetheless, outside of the caves, his anxiety continued to grow until – as we'd say in the West – he had full-blown panic disorder.

In desperation, Mingyur Rinpoche got up the courage to ask whether he could study formally with his father, Tulku Urgyen. His father agreed and began to teach him various methods of meditation. As it was with the solo chanting, this led Mingyur Rinpoche to experience brief moments of calm, yet his dread and fear persisted. He found it especially stressful that every few months he was sent to Sherab Ling monastery in India to study with unfamiliar teachers, among unfamiliar students. Plus, there was his formal enthronement as the seventh incarnation of Yongey Mingyur Rinpoche.

"Hundreds of people attended the ceremony," he's written,

"and I spent hours accepting their gifts and giving them bless-
ings, as if I were somebody really important instead of just a
terrified twelve-year-old boy. As the hours passed, I turned so
pale that my older brother, Tsoknyi Rinpoche, who was standing
beside me, thought I was going to faint."

About a year later, Mingyur Rinpoche learned that a three-
year retreat was soon to take place at Sherab Ling and it would be
led by Saljay Rinpoche, a renowned master. Mingyur Rinpoche
was thirteen – an age considered too young for such intense
practice – but he suspected that this would be the last three-year
retreat that the elderly Saljay Rinpoche would ever lead. Mingyur Rinpoche begged his father for permission to participate,
and, in the end, permission was granted.

"I'd like to say that everything got better once I was safely
settled among the other participants in the three-year retreat,"
Mingyur Rinpoche has admitted. "On the contrary, however,
my first year in retreat was one of the worst of my life. All the
symptoms of anxiety I'd ever experienced – physical tension,
tightness in the throat, dizziness, and waves of panic that were
especially intense during group practices – attacked in full force.
In Western terms, I was having a nervous breakdown. In hind-
sight, I can say that what I was actually going through was what
I like to call a 'nervous breakthrough.'"

Mingyur Rinpoche had to make a choice between spending
the last two years of the retreat cringing in his room or fully accepting the truth of what he'd learned from his teachers – that
whatever problems he was experiencing were habits of thought
and perception.

Mingyur Rinpoche chose what he'd been taught and gradually, just by sitting quietly and observing, he found himself able
to welcome his thoughts and emotions, to become in a sense, fascinated by their variety and intensity. It was like "looking through
a kaleidoscope and noticing how the patterns change," he wrote
in *Joyful Wisdom*. "I began to understand, not intellectually, but
rather in a direct, experiential way... how thoughts and emotions

that seemed overwhelming were actually expressions of the infinitely vast and endlessly inventive power of my own mind."

Mingyur Rinpoche has never had another panic attack, nor has his sense of confidence and well-being wavered. That's not to say, however, that he no longer experiences any ups and downs. He is careful to say that he isn't enlightened, and he's forthright about being subject to the full range of ordinary human experiences, including feeling tired, angry, and bored. What is different is that his relationship to these experiences has permanently shifted; he's no longer overwhelmed by them.

According to Cortland Dahl, Mingyur Rinpoche's panic attacks led him to begin practicing and studying the dharma in a very atypical way for a lama – a way much closer to how we in the West approach it. He believes that one of the reasons that Mingyur Rinpoche's teachings resonate so much with Western students is his willingness to talk about his own personal challenges.

"For cultural reasons," Dahl explains, "lamas are happy to talk about other people's issues, yet they don't typically talk about their own struggles with practice or emotions. Yes, he was a *tulku*, a reincarnate lama, and yes, he grew up in this amazing environment with a family of great teachers. But he studied the dharma not only because that's the typical training of a young tulku, but because he desperately needed it. He really wanted to find a way to work through this painful episode in his life.

"In a similar way, a lot of us in the West have come to Buddhism because we're suffering and we want some way to work with our minds. Mingyur Rinpoche can really speak to our experience in a very direct way. It's not only that he went through it, but that he is candid about it."

In a world that equates happiness with big-ticket items, Mingyur Rinpoche stands in stark contrast. Even before leaving the monastery with just the clothes on his back, he had an ultra-simple life. Extremely health conscious, he didn't eat any meat or refined sugars and he jogged every day. *He jogged in old penny loafers.* Once, some people wanted to buy him some sneakers, but his response was, "Thank you, but I don't need them – they won't fit in my bag." The one bag he carried with him when he traveled was that tiny.

"Everything Mingyur Rinpoche gets," says Cortland Dahl, "all the donations and the money from his books, goes to his monasteries or dharma projects. People were always coming in and giving him gifts and offerings, but usually he gave whatever it was to the next person that came in. He has literally next to nothing."

He was sixteen when he came out of his first three-year retreat, and much to his surprise he was appointed master of the very next one. This made him the youngest known lama to ever hold this position. It also meant that he was, effectively, in intensive retreat for almost seven continuous years.

Attending a monastic college, serving as the functioning abbot of Sherab Ling Monastery, taking full ordination vows as a monk – Mingyur Rinpoche's young adulthood was extremely busy. It was 1998 before he was able to delve into a branch of learning that he'd been interested in for years. Science.

As a child, he knew Francisco Varela, a world-renowned neuroscientist who'd come to Nepal to study Buddhism with Tulku Urgyen Rinpoche. Varela frequently talked to Mingyur Rinpoche about modern science, especially in regard to the structure and function of the brain. Other Western students of Tulku Urgyen gave him informal lessons in biology, psychology, chemistry, and physics.

"It was a little bit like learning two languages at the same time," Mingyur Rinpoche has written. "Buddhism on the one hand, modern science on the other. I remember thinking even then that there didn't seem to be much difference between the two." They were both methods of investigation.

In 2002 he was one of the advanced meditators invited to the Waisman Laboratory for Brain Imaging and Behavior at the

University of Wisconsin–Madison, where scientists examined the effects of meditation on the brain. Major publications such as *National Geographic* and *Time* reported on the results of the groundbreaking research. Notably, while the adepts meditated on compassion, neural activity in a key center in the brain's system for happiness jumped by 700 to 800 percent. In the control group, made up of people who'd just begun to meditate, activity increased by only 10 to 15 percent. Meditation, the study suggested, had the potential to increase happiness.

Early in 2009, Mingyur Rinpoche let his retreat plans be known to a small circle of people, the people who – as Dahl puts it – would "keep the ship afloat" in his absence. After he left, his brother Tsoknyi Rinpoche explained during a July 2011 retreat at Garrison Institute that "Mingyur Rinpoche wanted to do retreat and he planned for it – he did not abandon his activities without responsibility. He recorded four to five years of instruction, he trained instructors, he fund-raised, and he delegated all his work. So, he prepared everything."

Then in the summer of 2010 in Minnesota, Mingyur Rinpoche made a formal public announcement about his retreat plans. People, however, assumed that he intended to take a closed three-year retreat – an assumption that makes sense, as choosing to be a wandering yogi is highly unusual, especially in modern times.

Why is practicing in this style now so rare?

According to Tergar instructor Tim Olmsted, after Tibetans fled their country in the '50s, both first- and second-generation lamas had to struggle to keep the Buddhist tradition alive. To build monasteries and monastic colleges, they needed to dedicate enormous amounts of time to raising money; they had to publish books and travel to the West and Southeast Asia to gather students. In short, the lamas simply never had the chance to be wandering yogis.

But there is another reason that wandering isn't common today: "It's hard," Olmsted says bluntly.

Myoshin Kelley, also a Tergar instructor, expands on that. "I don't think many of us are ready for a wandering yogi retreat," she says. "To have some walls around us, a consistent food supply, and a safe environment to meditate in is a great support, which frees up a lot of energy that we can then direct toward looking deeply into our hearts and minds. For wandering yogis, there is a huge level of uncertainty that they have to deal with on a daily basis. That uncertainty could make it harder to maintain the stable mind that allows for realization. I see being a wandering yogi as an advanced practice."

Annabella Pitkin, a Columbia University professor who has done extensive research on renunciates and wandering yogis, agrees it's advanced, but that doesn't mean all advanced practitioners wander or should wander. In the Tibetan tradition, there are many valid and powerful paths, she says. Realization is possible whether one is a monastic in an institution, a householder, a hermit recluse, or a wandering yogi. These broad categories are not even so clearly defined. For example, continues Pitkin, "One of the things that you often see in the Tibetan tradition is that people will be monks or nuns in an institutional setting at one point in their lives, maybe early on, then they'll leave and be wanderers. And eventually they'll start to stay in one place because they are teaching so much more." That said, even monastics who spend their whole lives in an institution do not have a cookie-cutter practice. For instance, some are ritual specialists, while others are administrators or teachers.

"There are lots of things that have to happen to keep the monastic tradition going," says Pitkin. And it's important to remember how critical it is that it *does* continue. Without the monastic tradition, she says, "there is no Buddhism, no continuity." At the same time, she asserts, in order to stay fresh, the tradition needs the inspiration offered by wandering yogis, those "figures of vivid passion that dramatically illustrate the totality of the Buddhist path."

In wandering, says Pitkin, "you renounce your attachment

to not just possessions and comfort, but to more subtle things, such as being famous and controlling where you go. As a wandering yogi, you go where circumstances dictate – you're responsive to the situations that you find yourself in. That is, there is total freedom from ordinary entanglements, but also a very profound renunciation of ordinary attachments.

"Renunciation is the core of the Buddhist path, so if the primary role of the lama is to teach others by giving talks, wandering practice helps them to do that, because it develops their own inner qualities. But lamas can also teach by way of demonstration, and being an exemplar of the renunciate lifestyle is a very powerful way to teach people to rethink their ordinary relationship to their lives and their possessions."

At the Garrison Institute in July, Sogyal Rinpoche, the author of *The Tibetan Book of Living and Dying*, spoke about Mingyur Rinpoche's retreat as a wandering yogi. "In the future, Sogyal Rinpoche said, "he'll be someone we all look toward as a guide and refuge."

Mingyur Rinpoche's close students knew he aspired to become a wandering yogi. What they didn't know was when he would leave. "I think that was very intentional," says Cortland Dahl. "Rinpoche obviously wants and wanted to be on his own. But it would have been next to impossible for him to do that if he'd actually told anybody when he was leaving. His Tibetan students – out of a mixture of devotion and caring and fear – would have forced an attendant on him."

The reverence accorded to wandering yogis in the Tibetan tradition is often in the abstract, says Pitkin. In practice, people don't generally want their own guru to leave, so the biographies of the wanderers are peppered with people trying to pin them in place. "It's great that Milarepa wandered," Pitkin quips, "but it's much better if *my* teacher stays here with me."

Mingyur Rinpoche is expected to wander for three to five years, possibly longer, and to come back in the same way he left. Without warning.

Meanwhile, Myoshin Kelley believes that Mingyur Rinpoche is spending or will spend at least part of his time in the mountains. "This is not only for his love of them," she says, "but because they are such a conducive environment for meditation. He has frequently told stories of yogis coming down from the cave to test their practice in the marketplace. Maybe he will first head for the mountains and then find his way to the chaos of a big city. Really, Mingyur Rinpoche could turn up anywhere and I find this a fun thought. Keep your eyes open and treat everyone as if they are your guru!"

There Is a Path that Frees Us from Suffering

A Profile of Gina Sharpe

B uddhist teacher Gina Sharpe once asked a student why she only attended meditation retreats that were specifically for people of color.

"Gina," the woman answered, "I'm from the South. If I'm the only black person in a room of ninety-nine white people, there's only one thing that's going to happen."

"What's that?" Sharpe asked.

Then came the woman's answer – graphic and powerful.

"A lynching," she said.

Looking back, Sharpe pinpoints this as the moment when she "really got it." While the white Buddhist community may be very sweet, very well-intentioned, that doesn't change people's visceral experience. "It was nothing I could argue with," Sharpe explains. "It's an emotional wound that won't heal."

Originally from Jamaica, Sharpe has white, black, and Chinese ancestry. "I'm so assimilated that I'm more comfortable than many people of color in a white world," she acknowledges. As a Buddhist practitioner in the Insight Meditation tradition, she never had any qualms about attending retreats that were otherwise all white, and for a long time she didn't entirely grasp how difficult it was for many people of color. Yet the first time she led a people of color retreat, she noticed an unfamiliar feeling of relaxation.

"I didn't realize that when I'm not in a diverse place, there's a certain amount of unconscious tension that I carry," she says. When she practiced with other people of color, the tension dropped away.

New York Insight is ten floors up on West 27th, but even from this height I can hear the sounds of Manhattan below – horns honking, music pulsing.

Gina Sharpe is at the front of the room wearing an understated gray top and black slacks. Previously a successful corporate lawyer, she was one of the center's cofounders seventeen years ago and is now its guiding teacher. To open her teaching, she taps a singing bowl, releasing a warm hum.

"We choose to spend our time together as a community," she says. "Even though we come together in what appears to be separate bodies contained in our own sacks of skin, we are inexorably connected. So, in that spirit, I ask you to turn to the people around you."

Reaching out my hand to greet my neighbors, I suddenly see what makes New York Insight unusual. Like so many convert Buddhist centers in North America, it has a clean look that is at once cheerful and spare. There are tidy rows of chairs and cushions, a pot of orchids, and a soothing statue of the Buddha. But unlike so many convert Buddhist centers, New York Insight has a diverse membership. Indeed, it looks like New York City itself – a vibrant mix of black, white, Asian, Latino.

While it might be tempting to think that this diversity happened automatically – a natural result of the center's urban, multicultural location – it is actually the product of years of effort.

According to Buddhist philosophy, ultimately there is neither black nor white; these are simply constructions of mind. But Buddhism also acknowledges relative truth, and it is true that there is a legacy of slavery in America and that racism is woven into the fabric of society.

"Given that," Sharpe tells me, "it's not just a matter of 'Let's put people in a room together and let them meditate and everything will be hunky-dory.' Work has to be done on all different fronts."

And that work starts with understanding structural racism. "What does structural racism really mean? It means it's not your fault," says Sharpe. "You're not to blame – you don't have to feel guilty – but you should recognize it as a problem that needs a solution. And how do we as Buddhists solve problems? The first thing we do is we sit down and try to see the truth."

Yet many Buddhists don't want to see that structural racism operates in their own communities. According to Sharpe, white Buddhists often believe they're so goodwilled that they can't possibly be racist, and this means that they can't be taught. Nobody wants to be seen as racist; nobody wants to look inside and see racist tendencies. "So, when you bring racism up," she says, "there's so much guilt and shame about it that *you* get shamed."

They're not coming. What's wrong with them? Why aren't they coming for these precious teachings that we have? This, according to Sharpe, is frequently the underlying attitude of predominantly white sanghas in regard to people of color not attending their centers. "There's a feeling of 'It's *their* issue, not *my* issue,'" she says. "But racism hurts everybody."

If it weren't for Duke Ellington, Gina Sharpe might still be in Jamaica.

Her mother was a legal secretary in Kingston, her father an alcoholic and womanizer. The couple divorced when Sharpe was five. Then a few years later, her mother decided to try to make a better life for her three daughters. Leaving them in the care of one of her former teachers, she immigrated to the United States, where she worked as a domestic servant – the only thing she could do under the radar.

Sharpe describes what happened to her as a Cinderella story. The teacher, who had a rather plain daughter, was cruel to the attractive Sharpe sisters. They were all supposed to have their own bedroom, but instead she piled them into one room and sometimes didn't give them any food to eat. Not wanting to add to their mother's burden, the girls did not tell her what was happening.

Finally, one of the sisters' school friends told her father about the situation, and he marched over to the teacher's house. "I'll talk to your mother later," he told the girls, "but you're coming with me now." He and his wife already had five children of their own, but they welcomed the Sharpes into their family.

Meanwhile, the girls' mother got married and acquired legal status in the U.S., yet she still couldn't send for her daughters because she didn't have enough money in the bank to satisfy the immigration requirements. But her new husband, a musician, was friendly with Duke Ellington. One day, Ellington caught her crying and asked what was wrong. After she explained the situation, he put the needed money into her bank account, and she immediately set to work on reuniting with her children.

Gina Sharpe, at age eleven, left her native land. Driving from the airport through Harlem, she was taken aback by the relentless expanse of towering buildings, the dirt, and the stark absence of nature. Yet she does not remember ever being homesick for Jamaica.

Sharpe had always excelled academically and, at her new school, a placement test landed her in ninth grade, making her three years younger than her classmates. Moreover, she was put into an experimental double-honors class for especially gifted students. It was like being at a private school, only without the price tag.

Sharpe was just fifteen years old when she entered Barnard, the prestigious women's college affiliated with Columbia, but the age difference between her and her classmates proved to be too much. Unprepared for the extracurricular activities of sex and alcohol, she dropped out after one year and got a job as a secretary and – briefly – as a model. She did not have to strike too many poses before concluding that models were treated like pieces of meat. Moving to the West Coast, Sharpe became an assistant to a movie producer and worked on the films *Little Big Man*, *Alice's Restaurant*, and *Paper Lion*. She introduced her sister Alma to the '60s sex symbol Troy Donahue and the two were married for a couple of years.

In 1970, Gina Sharpe returned to Barnard and completed her degree in philosophy with a minor in psychology. As it happened, on the day of her graduation Duke Ellington was across the street at Columbia. Though she did not speak with Ellington, Sharpe sat in the audience and watched as he was awarded an honorary degree.

Night has fallen, and through the windows at New York Insight all I see is darkness speckled with light shining from other windows near and far.

Tonight, Sharpe is offering a few Buddhist meditation pointers, which are in essence all about being at ease without collapsing. I try to "breathe the breath" as she recommends, and then she shifts into what she calls "the underpinning of the practice" – the Buddhist teachings.

About her meetings with students, Sharpe says, "I want to understand how the practice is manifesting in their life and thinking, because I believe that practice should permeate everything. It shouldn't be that you sit for forty-five minutes or an hour in the morning, and then you get up and there's no more thought of it. In every moment, there's a dharma lesson."

So when a student comes to Sharpe with a real-life concern such as "My mom is dying," Sharpe's response is twofold. First there is the simple human piece, which is, "Oh my God, your mom's dying. How are you and how is she?" Then Sharpe shifts into her role as a teacher, leading her student to explore deeper questions in the vein of: How does impermanence work in your life? What was your relationship to your mom? Are you holding resentment toward her and have you worked with that from the point of view of suffering and the end of suffering? Sharpe may point students in a certain direction, but, she says, "The student is wise enough to get it. I don't have to lend my wisdom because they've got their own wisdom that they can work with."

Sharpe's approach leading tonight's dharma talk is similar. In fact, as she puts it, it's not so much that she's leading a dharma talk but rather that we're all creating the talk together. The format is inquiry, and it's not a one-way street.

A woman sitting cross-legged on her chair takes the mike and explains that she's been meditating consistently for quite a while and she can feel how the practice has transformed her life. Yet, she says, "I have a hard time with actually landing on the teachings. They don't stick."

"What do you mean?" Sharpe probes.

"Like the four noble truths. I've heard them a million times, but every time it's like, 'Oh yeah, that's what they are!' Somehow I'm not super connected to them."

"Is it okay?"

The woman adjusts her hat. For her, she says, it's okay. Yet she wonders if it *really* is. She's just happy doing what she's doing. Shouldn't there be a next step?

Sharpe pauses. "So, what can I do for you?"

"I love your questions!" The woman smiles. "I guess the question is … I mean … you don't know me well enough to give me the answer on a personal level."

"Even if I did, I probably wouldn't!" Sharpe laughs. "Everybody learns differently. Maybe you don't need to know what the four noble truths are."

The woman persists: "Is it important to find a teacher?"

"Is it important to you?"

"I guess I'd want to have a reflection at some point."

"When it becomes a heart's desire – if it ever does – then you look for a teacher." But for now, Sharpe asks, what are other ways to seek the answers to life's big questions?

"There's a lot," the woman says. "Meditation is one."

"Beautiful."

"Therapy, friendships."

"Beautiful."

"Nature."

"Go for it!" says Sharpe. "Live your life fully. It doesn't have to look like anybody else's."

There is skillful means in Sharpe's teaching. It's not one size fits all. When a man in a grass-green shirt and glasses asks a related question, she gives a much more tempered, traditional response.

The man, who identifies himself as Ken, explains that he appreciates how meditation focuses the mind. Yet he's unclear how this leads to what he defines as the larger objectives of meditation: developing compassion and understanding no-self and impermanence.

"How long have you been practicing?" Sharpe asks him.

"For a few years but not consistently. Sometimes I give it up."

"Have you ever been on a silent retreat?"

"No, but I try to go to dharma meetings about three times a week, here and at Tibet House and the Shambhala Center."

"So where do you think you're falling short?"

Ken simply repeats that he isn't seeing the connection between meditation and wisdom.

Sharpe asks, "Are you interested in being able to think it through, or are you interested in being able to see it work its way into your life?"

"I'd like to know the intellectual connection."

"Aha! Well, there's a lot to be said for being able to reflect – we're intellectual beings. But we're also emotional and physical beings. The way to realize these connections is not by thinking them through."

Take the concept of impermanence, she tells him. You can watch the shifting tides and the spinning hands on a clock and you can tell yourself 150,000 times that everything is impermanent. Yet that doesn't mean you understand it in your gut.

As Sharpe sees it, the teachings of the different schools of

Buddhism all wind up in the same place: the four noble truths. Nonetheless, if we're all over the place in our practice, shopping around and sampling different traditions, we may have breadth but not depth. When we choose a path and delve into it deeply, our intention is not like a cork bobbing on the water but like a stone dropping down: the mind steadies and insight appears.

"If you've been practicing for a while, a retreat is really helpful," says Sharpe. On retreat, you get a base of stillness and silence, which broadens and deepens your practice at home.

"Then insight is nothing that you have to seek," she concludes. "It simply happens. The mind is still and so it sees the nature of reality, and, from that, wisdom and compassion arise. When we see for ourselves that we are deeply connected to other beings, we don't have to try to be compassionate. Compassion arises because we know there's no difference between us. Your sadness is my sadness; your joy is my joy. Meditation is a way of helping the mind settle so it understands that in a deep way."

Gina Sharpe's home is full of buddhas. There's a white one presiding over the kitchen where her husband, John Fowle, is making lunch. Then there's a buddha of gilded wood in the piano room and one of brass in the bedroom. And hanging on the living room wall there's a Chinese painting on tin of an arhat. Thirty-five years ago, Sharpe tells me, she was going up an escalator in Bloomingdale's when she saw this arhat and decided he had to be rescued from just being somebody's decoration. For Sharpe, Buddhist imagery is a tangible reminder to practice. She smiles when she puts it this way: "Lest you forget."

Fowle serves lunch in the dining room and the three of us cluster at one end of a long table. In the center, there's a South African table runner decorated with a giraffe motif, and at our feet there's a cat with a charmingly strident meow. The meal is a carrot-mushroom medley, perfectly seasoned asparagus, and brown rice topped with a kidney bean stew. Though I relish every bite, Fowle insists that his wife is the better cook.

The couple met more than three decades ago when they were both young lawyers – Fowle working for a firm in the Bahamas and Sharpe working for another in New York. Their first date was at a restaurant that served platters of sizzling steak, and Fowle says he was so nervous that he invited a friend along. "This particular friend was married to a brain surgeon, and he told me not to get involved with Gina because she was too smart. I totally ignored his advice."

Less than two years later, on an afternoon in September, Fowle and Sharpe went to Tiffany's and picked out a ring. The next day they got married.

I ask Sharpe how she and her husband find equilibrium in their relationship, and her answer is generosity and kindness. According to Sharpe, marriage is difficult because it's a very close relationship with someone who has their own practice, their own history, and their own ideas about how things should be. We all have a history of trauma, isolation, and abandonment, and so much of what constitutes life is how our past difficulties manifest and how we work with that. Marriage, she says, is not just about "How do I get my needs met?" It's about "How do I get my needs met? How does the other person get their needs met? And how does the relationship, which is a third entity, get what it needs?"

"A marital relationship," says Sharpe, "shows you all of the places where you're stuck, all of the places where you're selfish. Marriage is the dharma of sex and money and work and relationship all contained in one situation. If we look at it as practice, then we learn from the conflicts that naturally arise."

As for Sharpe and Fowle, I've rarely encountered a couple so supportive of each other. When I ask Fowle who his teacher is, he tells me there's a group: Sharon Salzberg, Joseph Goldstein, and Jack Kornfield. But his number one is his wife.

"This is clearly biased," he says. "I don't care. Gina is the best there is. What I love about Gina's teachings is that they can cover a Buddhist text and be very detailed, and then she'll open it up and take you from your head to your heart." Fowle also points to the work that Sharpe has done for people of color in the dharma.

"It's not about proselytizing to those 'poor people of color' who need to know the dharma," she explains. "When we're in a room that's not diverse, we're missing opinions, we're missing viewpoints of the world. So getting a more diverse sangha is about enriching our community. It's not about getting them to come get what we've got but for them to bring with them what they've got. When we all study the dharma together, it becomes really rich."

Sharpe feels that a critical step to encourage diversity is retreats and sitting groups specifically for people of color. In these safe spaces, people of color have the opportunity to connect with Buddhist practice and many of them will fall so in love with it that they'll then begin attending general retreats and sitting groups.

In 2005, Sharpe was instrumental in establishing the NYI People of Color Sangha, a sitting group that meets once a month. This was followed by other initiatives to reach out to people of color and to educate convert Buddhists, particularly those in leadership positions, about issues of race, diversity, and equity.

Recently, Sharpe and her collaborators launched "Cultivating a Beloved Community," an eight-week course that explores differences and similarities through a Buddhist lens. The first course was led by four teachers – a white lesbian, a black gay man, a white straight man, and a black straight woman – and forty-five people applied for the sixteen available spots. "It's not just talking about race or sexual orientation or prejudice," says Sharpe, "but is really looking at suffering and the end of suffering."

"The way suffering ends," she concludes, "is that its cause is understood. Racism is a huge part of American suffering. If we're not attending to it, we're being ignorant."

Right from the Beginning

A Q&A with Raffi

When I was in elementary school I had a dog named Raffi, and people were always asking me, "Did you name him after the children's singer?" I didn't, though that would have been quite the honor for my furry family member. Raffi Cavoukian, better known as simply Raffi, made his first album in 1976 and it quickly went gold. More albums followed and he became – as described by *The Washington Post* – "the most popular children's entertainer in the Western world." But now Raffi has changed tracks and, as a systems thinker, he has founded a center in British Columbia for advancing what he calls "child honoring." In a recent conversation with Raffi, we talked about what child honoring means, how to put it into practice, and what has changed about childhood in the past three decades.

What qualities do children have that adults should try to cultivate in themselves?

There are many qualities – a playful nature is one. Play is the universal language of childhood and is, I think, an intelligence. Also, children are honest. Their love is pure. They don't ask anything but that you love them and that you be true to who you are with them. There's a divine essence to being human, and it's most visible in the child. They are playful, curious, wondering, purely loving. They have their own sense of the bodhisattva in them.

Your philosophy, child honoring, has what you call three givens.

Yes, child honoring stresses that the early years are the

foundational time of life. This is when we form our view of self and our view of the world. So, that's number one. Number two is that we live at a time with unprecedented global crises – a number of which could bring civilization to its knees – and all these crises in the world affect children the most. Children have the most to gain or the most to lose by the world we make for them. Number three is that the unprecedented scope and scale of the world's problems needs a remedy of equal scale, so what's called for is a whole-systems shift of our institutional values. That's why I call child honoring the compassion revolution – it really does involve a revolution in values in every sector.

You wrote a covenant for honoring children.

The inspiration for the covenant came from the Declaration of Independence. I looked at the Declaration to see if there were references to children. Of course, there aren't any – there aren't any references to women either. It was written in the 1700s. So, I thought, what would a similarly spirited emancipatory piece on children have to say and that's when I started writing the covenant – three paragraphs that are a direct affirmation of the child. Then a year later I wrote the principles. There had to be something to hang your hat on and the nine principles taken together proffer a way of living. The covenant and its principles form the core of the child honoring philosophy.

Can you give us a taste of the covenant?

The first sentence says a lot. It says, "We find these joys to be self-evident: That all children are created whole, endowed with innate intelligence, with dignity and wonder, worthy of respect." That much gives you a taste of the covenant and that also leads to the first principle, which is respectful love.

Twice you've talked with the Dalai Lama and discussed child honoring. What does he think about it?

The Dalai Lama has been very affirming. As an ecology advocate, he understands that how we take care of this planet affects children's lives directly. He also understands that it's not just the physical environment that's important, but the emotional environment of the home as well. All of the environments that we create for children must be imbued with good cultural values.

For years, the Dalai Lama has said that the world needs a universal ethic for the world's billions, regardless of religion. Child honoring is one clear expression of such an ethic, because the child is the most universal human experience. Everyone was once a child, even if they don't have any of their own. What better way to express a universal ethic than with the universal aspect of being human?

The Dalai Lama and I are on the same page about, as he calls it, "right from the beginning." In other words, we believe in imparting good cultural values right from the start, not later on when people are forty and they're in a workshop. The proactive engagement of the child right from the beginning is the most effective way of growing the very virtues that we wish to see in the world.

What's one special memory you have of your time with the Dalai Lama?

He was so sweet. When he said that even before birth we should start imparting good values, he pointed to his own abdomen, as though he were a mother. He totally gets the mother-child connection as the most important connection of all.

What made you decide to start singing for kids?

It was my good fortune many years ago to be married to a kindergarten teacher, and during that time I was asked to come into the classroom to sing for children. That led to the making of my first album and then a whole career opened up. I embraced it when I came to understand the importance of music for children.

What are the messages in your songs?

A song called "All I Really Need" is about the basics of life – good food, clean water and air. "One Light, One Sun" talks about the one world that nourishes all of us – the one light warming everyone. There have been many songs that give thanks for the world we have. There is a song called "Thanks A Lot" on the *Baby Beluga* album, and it's a song of gratitude. "Baby Beluga" itself, my best-known song, is essentially a love song for a magnificent creature. There have been messages of universal love in many, many songs.

You started singing for children in 1974. How has childhood changed since then?

Children – their basic needs – haven't changed. The world around them has. We have more telecommunications now, and television, unfortunately, has a bigger presence in children's lives. Also, in the polluted world that we have created, the body burden of toxic chemicals that is in our blood is quite something. There are trace amounts of toxic chemicals in most people's blood around the world and this is a new thing. Now we have this untenable situation where every child is born at risk of exposure to toxic chemicals in their body. This is what we must turn around. If we do, it will benefit all of us.

I understand that you've refused all commercial endorsement offers and Troubadour Music, your company, has never directly advertised or marketed to children.

Children deserve the best from us – they deserve the highest consideration as impressionable people. But corporations exploit children to become lifelong consumers. I'm thinking of the direct advertising to children in Canada and the United States. In Quebec and also the Scandinavian countries, that's illegal – you're not allowed to advertise to children twelve and under.

Is there anything you'd like to add?

I know child honoring is a big idea, but it's a very simple idea that, if taken seriously, can change our societal values and reorder our priorities in the direction of a world fit for children, a world in which our spirit can do its best work.

Does My Dog Have Buddhanature?

Exploring the Dharma of Dogs

In one of the Jataka Tales, the traditional stories about the Buddha's previous lives, there is a great black hound. This gigantic beast – as dark as midnight and with four fangs the size of bananas – has one purpose: terrifying people into right action.

My childhood dog, Raffi – a white poodle-Lhasa Aspo mix – was no great black hound making the world right. And, yet, he thought he was. With his surprisingly guttural woof, Raffi struck fear into anyone who had the audacity to ring the doorbell, and if the German shepherd next door stepped paw onto our property, Raffi ran her off. (Why did she flee from a dog less than half her size? Possibly because she was confused by the incongruity of his ferocity and lamb-like looks. *Surely, he must have some nasty canine tricks up his sleeve.*)

But Raffi – full name Raphael Tubs – was even more than the cosmic police dog of his imagination. For me, he was something of a dharma teacher and he helped me see that every dog is. If you rub their bellies and scratch their ears, they give their teachings freely.

Buddhist teachers of the human variety often assert that all beings have the same basic desire for happiness. Living with a dog takes that teaching out of the realm of the theoretical and makes it real.

We all want love: When two people hugged, Raffi would get jealous and yap. He wanted to be included in any show of affection. *We all need nourishment:* As an adult, Raffi mostly ate dry dog food, but no matter where he was in the house, he came running if someone took Cheddar out of the fridge. Raffi did not care for bacon and was refined enough that even if you put a roast beef on the floor, he wouldn't go near it unless you invited him to. (He was very keen to receive such an invitation.) *We all want to be safe:* If Raffi felt like he was in danger, such as whenever he was in a room where there was a man wearing a hat, he always barked furiously. Raffi, like so many us, had a tendency to lash out if he felt insecure. *We all want to be warm and dry:* Raffi would not go for a walk when it was raining hard. His little green coat did nothing to change the situation.

I don't know anyone who shares a bed with an octopus or who is greeted daily at their door by a wombat. Unlike almost any other animal, dogs live happily and intimately with humans, so dogs can be our door to understanding that all sentient beings have the same essential wants and needs. If we are open to understanding that all beings suffer and that all beings want to be happy, our compassion deepens, widens. This is the compassion chain: from dog, it's no great leap to wolf, and from wolf it goes from fox to weasel to bobcat and on and on.

Yet not everyone is willing to see that all beings suffer and that all beings want happiness. Even a lot of people with a canine teacher curled at the foot of their bed don't want to admit that dogs have so-called human feelings; they believe this anthropomorphizes them.

But I am not anthropomorphizing. Let me assure you, Raffi was decidedly a dog. He loved gnawing on bones and sticking his head out the car window – the wind blowing back his ears. Moreover, unfixed, he was a complete horn dog, keen to hump male dogs, female dogs, and stuffed animals. Once (oh, the horror!) he even tried to mount a human baby who'd just learned to crawl.

Raffi's dog-ness brings me to that most famous of doggie questions, the first koan in the *Gateless Gate* collection and the first koan that's usually given to Zen students:

A monk asked Chao-chou, "Does a dog have buddhanature or not?"

Chao-chou said, "Mu."

The monk must have been familiar with the Buddha's teaching that all creatures have buddhanature, but intellectual familiarity doesn't mean that he had actually realized the truth of it. Doubting a dog's buddhanature was of a piece with doubting his own. After all, if a dog's dog-ness makes it too base for buddhanature, then surely our humanness makes us too base as well.

Not in the business of debate or philosophizing, Zen master Chao-chou gave the monk a stripped-down response: "Mu," meaning *no thing, nay,* or *no.* Linguistically, a complete negative.

But that doesn't make sense! The response was contrary to the Buddha's teachings: *We all have buddhanature.* So how to make sense of it? Don't use intellect; forget that big human brain.

"If," said the late American Zen teacher Robert Aitken, "you are preoccupied with 'has' and 'has not,' that is, if you cultivate thoughts about attaining something, you cut off your head, or rather you cut off your body. You cut off the whole world. Preoccupied with brooding, fantasy, memory, or whatever, you are unable to hear the thrush in the avocado tree."

Rinzai master Koryu Osaka (1901-1987) put it another way: "Mu itself is the buddhanature, and when you thoroughly make this your own, in that moment, you realize what you are. If you fall into the sphere of dualism, even just a little bit, then you lose sight of it, you completely lose the total of this koan."

But Raffi did not grapple with koans. He had no need. He had already realized his true doggie nature..

My mother would dedicate Saturday afternoon to bathing him with blueing shampoo and blowing him dry. Then, almost immediately, he'd slip into the backyard where there was a lake – a cool inviting mirror of water – and he would just plunge in, ruining his freshly clean coat. Raffi lived in the moment. When chasing a ball, just chase. When barking at the TV, just bark.

And moment by moment, Raffi changed. That was his final lesson; everything is of the nature to change. Impermanence, according to the Buddha, is one of the marks of existence, and dogs don't generally live as long as humans, so loving them is a teaching.

When he came into my life, Raffi could fit in my hands and

his nose was pure pink. Over time, he went from very small to not as small, and his nose went from pink to marbled pink and brown and then finally to pure brown. He got liver spots. He lost an eye to cancer, and eventually he was diagnosed with a cancer that couldn't be cured.

When I was twenty-three and about to move to Japan for a year, I took my time one day holding and petting Raffi. I knew that he was old and might not be alive by the time I got back. As it turned out, I was right; Raffi was put down while I was away.

My mother snipped off a lock of his fur for me to keep and then she buried him in the far corner of her property. Later, though, she realized that she didn't actually own that land; a neighbor did. Briefly, she considered digging him up and moving him, then she decided that he was exactly where he was supposed to be. In life, Raffi loved bolting off and exploring every yard and road and wild space. It's fitting that, even now, he still cannot be fenced in.

Wise Guy

A Profile of Michael Imperioli

Christopher Moltisanti walks into a bakery to buy pastries for his Mafia boss. He takes a number – thirty-four – and waits for what feels like half of New Jersey to get served. Then Christopher's number comes up and he's about to order when Gino, yet another customer, walks through the door. The clerk, talking past Christopher, asks Gino what he can get for him.

"Whoa," says Christopher, slamming the counter. "Number thirty-four right here."

"He was in line," says the blond clerk. "He just went out to get gas in his car."

"Oh, so I can go out, fuck your sister, come back Saturday – I go to the front of the line?"

"I said he could." The clerk's tone is harder than week-old bread.

"Hey, poppin' fresh," says Christopher. "I'm in no fucking mood today. I'm next. Now get a fucking pastry box."

But still the clerk turns to Gino and insists on serving him, even when Gino says it's okay, that Christopher can go ahead of him. So Christopher opens the bakery door for Gino. "Take a walk," he says. Then Christopher flips the open sign to closed and whips out his gun. "What is it? Do I look like a pussy to you? … I'm serious – be honest. I won't get mad."

"No," stutters the clerk. "I'm sorry."

"Get a pastry box," says Christopher. Then, when the clerk doesn't hop to it fast enough, he shoots the floor close to the clerk's feet. The clerk quickly fumbles for the box and fills it with cannoli, sfogliatelle, and napoleans. He closes the lid and hands the box to Christopher.

"Next time you see my face," Chris says, now so softly, so calmly, "show some respect."

"I will," the clerk says.

Then, just when both the clerk and viewers are breathing a sigh of relief, Christopher shoots the clerk.

"You motherfucker," he shrieks. "You shot my foot."

"It happens," says Christopher, already on his way out the bakery door.

But that's television, a scene from the first season of *The Sopranos*. In real life, Michael Imperioli, the actor who played mobster Chris, is a thoughtful Tibetan Buddhist.

In an interview, I ask Imperioli how he reconciles his Buddhist beliefs about compassion with the violence in *The Sopranos* and other shows he's been in. Hopefully, he tells me, "you'll be revolted by it and you'll realize it's deluded to think that's a justifiable way of living your life." If you're going to show a mob character, he continues, "it's important to show him in a graphic way because otherwise, when you're laughing with him and you see him with his wife, you'll relate to him and maybe start to think something like 'oh, he's just another father.' So you have to see that flip side – the cruelty and the dehumanizing of the victims – to realize who these people are and to realize that it's a very destructive and unkind way of life. It's more truthful to present both sides than to clean it up."

Buddhism can help an actor understand characters – to understand their point of view and motivation – and to develop compassion for them. Imperioli says it's important that he not judge the characters he plays as bad or evil because, once he does, he's looking at them from an outside point of view. Bad and evil are labels, he says, "and have nothing to do with the internal mechanisms of what drives a character, which is what I'm going to need to get in touch with in order to play him. And, you know, even the worst people probably think they're good in some ways. There's something motivating them."

Both real-life Michael Imperioli and fictional Christopher

Moltisanti are screenwriters – Imperioli having written, among other things, several episodes of *The Sopranos* and having co-written Spike Lee's *The Summer of Sam*. But Imperioli laughs when I ask in what other ways he's similar to Christopher. "Not many, I hope," he tells me. "I mean, Chris tried really hard. He tried hard to be good at what he did, both as a mobster and as a screenwriter. Not everybody who has an idea for a movie actually sits down and writes the script. He actually did it. He was diligent and I think I share that, but he had a lot of rough qualities. He was a very selfish person. I have been that at times, hopefully, though, less and less as I get older."

Michael Imperioli, born in 1966, grew up in a working-class, Italian American neighborhood in Mount Vernon, New York. His father was a bus driver and amateur actor; his mother was a secretary. The family was Catholic.

"I felt a connection to the teachings of Christ and the life of Christ," Imperioli says, "but I really didn't like going to church. Like most kids, I just felt bored."

More to his childhood tastes were biblical movies – *The Ten Commandments, King of Kings, The Greatest Story Ever Told*. The message was compassion and love, Imperioli says, and he liked seeing these values promoted. It inspired him to see characters on the screen face obstacles and overcome them.

In his teens, Imperioli stopped going to church, and though he didn't pursue it, he began to feel the draw of Buddhism. He was haunted by the images of Vietnamese monks setting themselves on fire in protest of the Vietnam War and he was fascinated by the work of Jack Kerouac and Allen Ginsberg. But in high school, Imperioli was also reading plays and resolving to have an acting career, so – immersed in theater and film – a decade was to go by before he explored spirituality.

Imperioli read about mysticism and the occult; he read Krishnamurti and Gurdjieff and Ouspensky. The first Buddhist book he read was *Meditation in Action*, by Chögyam Trungpa Rinpoche. "In my late twenties," says Imperioli, "I was what

Trungpa Rinpoche would call a spiritual shopper. I would read books and they would all make sense to me and I'd get a lot out of them. But a couple of days later, after I'd finished them, I'd be back in my old habitual patterns and habitual way of thinking. It wasn't until I had a real practice, which I got through Buddhism, that I felt things starting to change."

In 1996, Imperioli married Victoria Chlebowski, a stage designer who had fled her native Ukraine with her mother in 1976 because of anti-Semitism. In college, she studied some philosophy and read a lot of Buddhist books, which she shared with Imperioli. Then about five years ago, the couple began attending Buddhist teachings in New York City, where they live. The first teachings they went to were by Gelek Rinpoche, who has been the teacher of such luminaries as Allen Ginsberg and Phillip Glass. Now Imperioli and his wife go to all of Gelek Rinpoche's teachings that they can manage, as well as to the teachings of Sogyal Rinpoche and the Dalai Lama. In July, they took refuge with Garchen Rinpoche.

"I always had a sense that spirituality meant having to work on yourself, rather than just adopting a set of beliefs and following them blindly," says Imperioli. "And the more I learned about Buddhism, the more I felt that's really what it is – direct methods of working on yourself, meditation being the first method. It made sense to me that the only way to transform your world was to transform yourself."

Imperioli and his wife have busy careers and three children, yet they've made practice a priority by cutting out the superfluous. "We live a low-profile life," Victoria Imperioli explains. "We have our circle of friends but we are very family-oriented. If we go to an event at all, we go to see someone's play or film. We never really go to parties. You can't fit in everything."

"Buddhism has brought a lot of benefit to our family," says Imperioli. "I see the change in my wife, because it's easier to see it in someone else. Patience, tolerance, peace of mind – these things have increased in her a lot. When you can see your partner being more patient and being kinder to herself, it inspires you. Those benefits are for the children as well."

The couple practices meditation in the morning, as well as shortly before bed, and Imperioli says that he doesn't find it difficult to fit practice into his schedule. The challenge is more procrastination. Sometimes he struggles to bring himself to the cushion or he struggles with runaway thoughts. At those times, he tells himself that it is his conditioned mind and to let it go and just sit. "I don't find practice ever to be easy, but that's okay," he says. "I can't say that I'm a 100 percent – there are times when I don't practice. I try to not let that happen too much and I try not to beat myself up about it when it does."

Meditation has benefited not only Imperioli's family life, but his work, specifically his concentration as an actor. "When you're acting or preparing to act," he says, "you want to focus your attention and block out distractions. It's not the same thing as meditation but the focus has similarities."

In an episode of the ABC crime drama *Detroit 1-8-7*, night has fallen and James Burke is in an apartment, holding his mother and children at gunpoint. Unarmed but wired, Detective Fitch, played by Imperioli, walks into the hostage scene.

"I know what it's like," says Fitch, with a whole SWAT team just outside the apartment, hanging on every word through the wire. "You love somebody so much. You don't know why they caused you so much pain ... that pain builds and builds ... It's like you're a passenger. You're in a car that's speeding out of control but then you wake up and it's *you* behind the wheel and it's *you* who did these things. I did things... I hurt my wife. I hurt my kids. When I think about the things I've done, sometimes I really think it'd be easier just to end it ... But I got these pictures on my wall. I see my kids – I can't do it."

Fitch pulls a photo out of his suit pocket. The smiling faces of Burke, his ex-wife whom he recently pumped full of bullets,

and their two children. "These are your kids, James, your beautiful kids."

Burke points his gun at Fitch. "Don't come any closer."

"Give me the gun, James."

"Stop," he chokes.

"I'm not gonna stop, James. Give me the gun." Fitch takes
the weapon; James sobs.

"God, forgive me," says James.

Later that night, Fitch is back at the office with his new
partner, Detective Washington, and they're looking at a white
board filled with murder cases. Washington's voice is soft. "All
that stuff you said ... is it true?"

Fitch shoots him a hard look. "It was true when I said it."

And that's how it is with Michael Imperioli. On screen,
when he says anything, it's true. When he says it.

I ask Imperioli how he does it – how he manages to make
his lines sound so real – even when he's been repeating them take
after take.

"You have to keep focusing on the elements of the scene and
the objective of the character," Imperioli says. "Every time you
do the scene, you have to take in the reality of what you're doing
and be in the moment. The most important thing for an actor is
to be in the moment."

After finishing high school, Imperioli studied method
acting in Manhattan at the Lee Strasberg Theatre and Film Institute. "The first thing they teach you is relaxation," Imperioli
tells me. "Basically, you sit in a chair and don't really do anything.
Then you might start adding sound or a physical movement."
You might work to recreate the physical sensations of holding
an object, such as a pencil or a cup of tea. The idea is to focus on
reliving the actual sensation, rather than simply miming what it
looks like to hold the object. When Imperioli thinks back on his
studies at Lee Strasberg, he sees a lot of similarities between the
techniques he learned and Vajrayana Buddhist practice, with its
visualizations and mantras.

"When I went to acting school," says Imperioli, "I thought that in a couple of months I'd start working on TV and be making all kinds of money – I was that stupid. It was four years before I got a part in a play, which didn't pay any money, and then another four years after that before I started making a living. If I had known how long it would take, I don't know if I would have done it."

While Imperioli waited for his break, he worked in restaurants; he was a waiter, busboy, bartender, and cook. Yeah, he believed he was going to make it. "But sometimes no," he admits. "There are times when you feel like it just might never happen. The reality is that there are a lot of good actors and you don't necessarily stand out that much. To succeed it takes a combination of being good and just persevering. Some luck doesn't hurt either." That said, according to Imperioli, it's not luck that someone gives you a part. It's luck that you don't get hit by a bus or get cancer, and that luck enables you to stick it out – if you have the perseverance in you. Eventually, he says, after you've done twenty plays and you've done a good job, someone knows you and gives you a small part in a film.

Michael Imperioli's first film credit is for John G. Avildsen's *Lean on Me*. After that, he landed other small parts in a variety of flicks, including Martin Scorsese's *Goodfellas*, Spike Lee's *Jungle Fever* and *Malcolm X*, Scott Kalvert's *The Basketball Diaries*, and Mary Harron's *I Shot Andy Warhol*. Then, in 1999, he got the part of Christopher Moltisanti in *The Sopranos*, the role he continues to be most known for and for which, in 2004, he won the Primetime Emmy Award for Outstanding Supporting Actor in a Drama Series.

For years, here and there, people on the street had recognized Imperioli and come up to talk to him, but *The Sopranos* took it up a notch – a big notch. "To be honest," he says, "it was a bit of an adjustment. When your privacy is invaded to a much bigger degree, it's a little strange trying to navigate that."

Suddenly finding himself in the limelight was one of the

reasons that Imperioli ended up delving into Buddhism. "In my twenties, pretty much all I cared about was acting," he explains. "I was driven to succeed, which you have to be to make it in the business." But what happened to Imperioli is what happens to a lot of people. "Finally, on some level," he says, "you achieve what's considered success. Then you realize it doesn't necessarily make you happy. So, if what you thought was going to be the ultimate thing to fulfill you doesn't actually make you happy, you better figure out what does."

"How can a path all about improving the self be about selflessness?"

Gus asks Lisette this question over a drink, his tone taking a sharp turn away from flirtation. They'd just met earlier in the evening, while she was outside having a smoke and he was ranting his poems into his cellphone. Now Gus presses on: "If I'm concerned with my life, my karma, my rebirth ... where's the sacredness in that?"

His anger jars against the bar's mellow music, the plaintive strains of guitar.

"What are you crying for?" he sneers. "You're crying 'cause you fear suffering. It's all about you. It's all about nothing."

"It's not," says Lisette. "The soul is not nothing."

"The truth is, sweetheart, there is no soul ... It's all up here." Gus strokes her head.

"Then what? We're all just ... bodies?"

Gus smiles. "It's the body, which is immortal. Now we're human and it's rotted into worms, which are eaten by birds, which are eaten by cats, which are eaten by dogs, who shit us out and we become grass, which is then eaten by cows who are milked and churned into cheese and swallowed in a cheeseburger by some teenager down at McDonald's and, hey, we're human once more, and on and on ... We're immortal."

Lisette weeps and Gus kisses her cheeks, cups her face in his hands. "Do you see the beauty in that?" he murmurs.

She nods weakly.

"Yes?" he persists, and she nods again. Then he traces her mouth with his thumb and slips the whole thing inside.

"Do you see the beauty in that?"

She sucks on one of his fingers. Then a second. A third. A fourth – her whole mouth stuffed. And still hungry.

Gus isn't played by Imperioli; rather Gus is his creation – a character from the 2009 film *Hungry Ghosts*, which was written and directed by Imperioli and produced by his wife. The title, which borrows from Buddhist cosmology, refers to beings with tiny mouths and huge, hungry stomachs; they try to consume but swallowing is excruciating and they can't get enough down their throats to satisfy. The film uses the term as a metaphor to describe people with a deep feeling of emptiness who try to fill themselves up by chasing their endless, illusory appetites – drugs, alcohol, sex, validation, sensation.

Imperioli wrote the script shortly after he started going to Buddhist teachings, yet the film is not Buddhist and neither are the characters in it, not even the guru character. Her spirituality is what Imperioli describes as a "hodgepodge," mostly a mix of Buddhism and Hinduism. "There are a lot of spiritual ideas that come into *Hungry Ghosts*," he says, "but it's really about spiritual confusion. It's about searching and not knowing what to search for, knowing you want something but not knowing what it is. I was inspired to write about those things from pursuing a spiritual path.

"I spent several years knowing that I had to start meditating but not doing it," says Imperioli. "I was convinced I couldn't."

Like many people, he believed that in order to meditate he had to stop thinking and he knew he wouldn't be able to do that. Eventually, however, he came to realize his misconception. What meditation actually involves is sitting down and acknowledging your thoughts.

Hungry Ghosts wraps up with meditation. That is, in the final scene, many of the principal characters meditate together, and right after Imperioli finished making the film, he started meditating himself. "So it's not a movie about Buddhism," he explains, "but in some ways it led to it."

Imperioli and his wife are working on a new film with a spiritual bent; they are executive producers of a documentary about the Tenzin Gyatso Scholars Program. This program, which sponsors Tibetan monastics to study neuroscience, biology, physics, and the social sciences in the United States, is a project of the Tenzin Gyatso Institute. Founded in 2007 by Sogyal Rinpoche, the institute strives to advance the Dalai Lama's vision and values, and the Scholars Program goes right to the heart of this mission. The Dalai Lama has frequently stated that science has enriched his views and that Tibetan religious education would benefit from a thorough understanding of how Western thought and inquiry has developed.

At the same time, says Imperioli, "masters meditating in caves thousands of years ago had insights that scientists are only now coming to terms with. The interrelation between physical science and Buddhism could help our view of the world."

When Imperioli tells me this, I think again of the characters in *Hungry Ghosts* and their search for meaning and happiness. In particular, I think of Gus and his raging question: "How can a path that is all about improving the self be about selflessness?" I ask Imperioli how he'd answer that.

"Gus is seeing that it's all about the self," says Imperioli. "He failed to make the leap toward making it really be about compassion and that's where he was limited."

Compassion and the importance of it is what Imperioli wants to leave his viewers with. "Compassion and the possibility of transformation," he says. "You can wake up."

I smile into the phone. Michael Imperioli's voice sounds just like Christopher Moltisanti's, but his words don't. Not at all.

What's Love Got To Do With It?

A Q&A with Tina Turner

When I was ten years old, I watched *Mad Max Beyond Thunderdome* and had my first glimpse of Tina Turner – her killer legs, impressively large shoulder pads (even by '80s standards), and the most incredible raspy, sexy voice I'd ever heard. What happened to me when I saw Turner on my TV screen is what, at that point, had been happening to audiences for more than two decades, and now has been happening for more than half a century: I was awed.

The Queen of Rock 'n' Roll is not just a powerhouse on stage. She is also a longtime Buddhist, having begun her practice in the 1970s while struggling to end an abusive relationship with musician Ike Turner. Soka Gakkai, the tradition to which Tina Turner adheres, is like other schools and subschools of Nichiren Buddhism; it focuses on the *Lotus Sutra* and teaches that chanting its title in Japanese – *Nam-myoho-renge-kyo* – ultimately enables chanters to embrace the entirety of the text and uncover their buddhanature.

Turner chanting the *Lotus Sutra* is featured on *Beyond*, a CD available through New Earth Records that weaves together Buddhist and Christian prayers, and also features the singers Dechen Shak-Dagsay and Regula Curti. "Bringing together corresponding pieces from Christian and Tibetan Buddhist traditions as has been done here," writes the Dalai Lama in the liner notes, "will allow listeners to share in these prayers, stirring thoughts of deeper respect and peace in their lives." All revenue from the CD goes to foundations dedicated to spiritual education or helping children and mothers in need.

In this interview, Turner speaks about *Beyond*, the power of song and practice, and the meaning of love.

All religions speak about love, and it sounds easy to be loving. But people so frequently fail to love. Why is loving so difficult?

Some people are born into a loving family. For example, everyone in the family greets everyone else in the morning, they sit at breakfast together, they give each other a kiss when they leave. There is harmony and love in the house. When you are born with that, you take it with you.

But some people are born into situations where they're exposed to everything *but* love. The world is full of people that are born into such situations, and they are traveling through life in the dark. No one has ever explained to them that they need to find love, and they have no education for love except for falling in love with another person, for sexual love. I believe that the problem with the world today is that we have too many people who are not in touch with true love.

What helped you to become loving?

When you don't come from your mother with love, you might have the gift to be surrounded by other people or situations that are loving and you learn to love in that way.

My mother didn't want a child, so I experienced being unwanted. But I found love when I was with myself. I would go into nature, into gardens and eat fruit. I would climb trees. I looked to nature and found love because love is in nature. If you go there, hurt and angry, it can transform you. I went with nature, with animals, and I found love and harmony. I would come home at the end of the day – braids pulled out, my dress torn – and of course I got asked, "Where have you been all day?" But I had been in a world of love and happiness.

I am very happy that I discovered love in nature because later I was in a relationship without love and I still found a way to find love. You can find love when you are of love.

Did singing help you?

I was singing almost from the moment I was born. Ever since I was big enough, I've been singing. When I was a little girl my mother would put me on a chair and I would sing for the shop ladies. So, I was born with a voice to sing and I have been singing all my life. It might be that being a singer helped me. Maybe singing on stage helped. Maybe it was a release.

In what way is singing a spiritual practice?

"Nam-myoho-renge-kyo" is a song. In the Soka Gakkai tradition we are taught how to sing it. It is a sound and a rhythm and it touches a place inside you. That place we try to reach is the subconscious mind. I believe that it is the highest place and, if you communicate with it, that is when you receive information on what to do. Singing a song can make you cry. Singing a song can make you happy. That's spirit – the spirit inside of you. If you look up "spiritual" in a dictionary, you will find that it is your nature, it is the person you are. When you walk into a room, a person might say, "Oh, she's got great spirit." Or you can walk into a room and someone will say that you don't have spirit because it's not visible. You're kind of off or negative. Meditation and praying change your spirit into something positive. If it is already positive, it makes it better. I think that is the best answer I can give you right now.

On Beyond, you say, "Sing – singing takes you beyond."

The singing that I am referring to on the CD is one that comes out of you when you hum. It's not necessarily a song;

rather it's that moment when you find yourself making sounds from within – from your heart, from your spirit. Each person has a musical song from their bodies. That is something I learned over time. You can play the tune of your name and this is the hum from inside of you that can give you peace when you are really down. My grandmother had a hum, never a song. She would hum sitting in a rocking chair and I would listen. As a singer, I wanted to know what my grandmother was singing. But it was the song of her soul. This song I am referring to is about singing, being happy, enjoying music, and even when you're depressed, still singing. You must try to find that sound or song within you. You might find that it is just a "huuuaa" or a "hum" or something in falsetto. But it is a sound, which comes out of you that gives you peace.

In what ways has your practice changed you?

I feel that chanting for thirty-five years has opened a door inside me, and that even if I never chanted again, that door would still be there. I feel at peace with myself. I feel happier than I have ever been, and it is not from material things. Material things make me happy, but I am already happy before I acquire these things. I have a nature within myself now that's happy. Practicing the words "Nam-myoho-renge-kyo" for so long has put me in another frame of mind, so that when I don't practice for a day or a week, I still feel happy. But I do practice.

Since I have been practicing Buddhism, I have to say I don't experience the feeling of guilt anymore. Practice clears the way. Chanting "Nam-myoho-renge-kyo" makes you comfortable because it removes uncomfortable mental attitudes. It doesn't just buy you a car or a house – it takes care of you.

What is your practice like? Do you ever include elements or practices from other Buddhist sects?

My practice these days is how I want it, how I feel it. I can take some time on weekends and just stay in my practice room and meditate, drink water, walk around. Depending on how busy I am, sometimes I go without practicing for a week and then I just click right back into it. I am not on the schedule of practicing precisely every morning and evening, but I consider myself a Buddhist. It is within me. Do I ever associate with other Buddhist elements? I haven't felt the need except when something comes to me directly. Since I've been living in Switzerland, I went to a shrine elsewhere in Europe and I've met His Holiness the Dalai Lama. Everybody knows I am a practicing Buddhist.

Would you say that you're still evolving spiritually?

Oh, I think as long as you are on this planet as a human being, you never get to the top of spiritual evolution. I think that you evolve until you leave the planet and you don't know how far you'll get until you leave.

You were born into a Christian family. Can you tell me about your transition from being a Christian to being a Buddhist?

I was born into a Baptist family. I went to church every Sunday. The preachers were speaking the words of God, but I didn't really hear what the preacher said. What affected me was the environment. It was the people's "amen" in agreeing with the preacher. We had a young Baptist reunion to learn about the Bible and it put me in touch with information about God and Jesus and being nice to people. My mother taught me that saying the Lord's Prayer would help me, so I kept saying it straight through life until I was introduced to Buddhism.

But it didn't matter that I changed from being a Baptist to being a Buddhist because I learned later that they're the same. They just use different words. Maybe I stopped saying the Lord's

Prayer and went into Buddhism because I needed new words – I needed refreshment – to get to the next step.

I noticed that saying the Lord's Prayer and chanting a mantra had a similar effect on me. But I was chanting a mantra for longer periods of time and more often than I had ever said the Lord's Prayer. I didn't have this system for the Lord's Prayer and it's a system that works for me.

Is it important to have a particular place to practice?

When I practiced the Lord's Prayer I simply went down on my knees, so you can pray anywhere, but there are psychological benefits when you have a shrine in a quiet place in your house where it is comfortable to sit. You can cry your heart out there and it is private. The fact is that you have to have your quiet place in your house, your Buddha shrine. It is not private at church where you have to listen to the priest. At your place, you are focusing on something your person and your mind needs.

In your view, how often do people need to practice?

Some people have to practice a lot – morning, middle of the day, evening. Some people can practice once a day. Traditionally, when you're starting out, you practice twice a day – when rising in the morning and before retiring in the evening. When I was having the hardest time of my life, I was practicing for four hours a day. And I saw how it was working. My reactions were spot on and I knew that was because of my practice, because my normal reactions weren't that way.

Why do you consider it important to have a CD that combines Buddhist and Christian prayers?

The answer to this question is unity. Years ago, when I was on tour in New Zealand, I was given a purple book that I couldn't stand the color of. But, somehow, I kept it and opened it after my tour. It explained that God is within us and it doesn't matter what your religion is. Whatever words you use, the results are the same. If you are in another country and you go to their meditation area to pray with them and you do your own prayer and they do theirs, that's fine.

The CD *Beyond* is to remind people or to educate people that God is inside them. How you tap into God is your decision. Whether you meditate or whether you become a Christian, it's up to you. *Beyond* is an invitation to open the heart for all religions and to become united.

How did you get involved with Beyond?

I was invited to get involved in the project by Regula Curti, born Christian in Switzerland, and Dechen Shak-Dagsay, born Buddhist in Tibet. I thought it was a good idea because I was already on the journey of unity, of thinking about how there are religious wars and how someone has to help people know that God is to be found within, so that peace and harmony will evolve.

Regula and Dechen and I started to chant together and we discovered unity on a deeper level, more energetically and spiritually. The thought of unity in prayer became, for all three of us, a field to explore musically. We hope that everybody realizes that the system – the system of God, of contacting God, of being a better person, and of correcting your life conditions – is within you. What we are trying to say is that it doesn't matter what holy words you chant, what matters is that you do it with all your involvement – physical, mental, spiritual. It doesn't matter if Regula sings Ave Maria and Dechen sings the prayer for Tara and I sing the *Lotus Sutra*. Prayer is prayer. What's important is doing it and not worrying about how others are praying.

On Beyond you say, "When you go beyond that's where you find true love." What does that mean to you? What is true love?

There are many different forms of love, but true love is something that transcends doubt, something that is not judgmental, something that is openhearted and accepting. We are not talking about passionate love, sexual love. We are talking about a love of human beings, of the planet – the love of seeing a little flower growing out of the earth at a certain time of the year.

If you have the capacity to find love in beauty, that is the door opener of true love. True love comes from looking at a beautiful day and the feeling that comes from that. Perhaps you don't have the words for it, but you just feel, "Ah, gosh, what a wonderful day," and that particular moment makes you happy. You see beauty and you embrace it – that is love.

What or where is this "beyond" that you refer to?

Oh, that's a deep question. Let's start with meditation. There is a stage in practice where you don't faint, you don't black out, but you are in a space. In this space you are able to stop the conscious mind, the one that constantly talks and gives you all kinds of information from your eyes, your ears, your nose. When you're able to get into that space, that is "beyond." That's where you find truth. In this stage of my life, I personally believe that you get truth from your subconscious mind and by meditating you get into the subconscious mind. Meditation opens the space I call "beyond."

What does it mean for you as a rock singer that your newest album is about prayer?

It means that people who work in the arts need prayer as much as anyone else. I don't separate my work as a rock singer from prayer. When I went on stage to make a living, I made people happy with my work. The feedback was always that I inspired people to get out and help themselves to go forward, to practice

Buddhism. Everything has been very positive and that's because of my spiritual practice.

I feel alone now – my mother is gone, my sister is gone. But I have two sons, I have my relationship with my partner, Erwin, and I have my practice. I feel that I have help. The practice takes care of me. If you practice, you will see that this is exactly what it does.

Four Keys to Waking Up

On Retreat with Pema Chödrön

About a year and a half before Ani Pema Chödrön teaches a program, she has to come up with a title for it. Now up on the stage at the Omega Institute in Rhinebeck, New York, she quips that she never knows so far in advance what she's going to teach, so she just comes up with something she figures she'll inevitably say something about. Her title for this weekend is "Walk the Walk: Working with Habits & Emotions in Daily Life."

As Ani Pema sees it, walking the walk is about being genuine; that is, not being a fake spiritual person.

"You got any idea what I mean by that?" she asks the retreatants. "One attribute that can be true of fake spiritual people is that they wear fake spiritual clothing," she says, taking a light crack at her own tidy burgundy robes. But what being a fake spiritual person really means, she explains, "is that you're suffering a lot and you want to mask your suffering with some kind of spiritual glow. You're trying to transcend the messiness of life by being beatific and radiant."

In contrast, Ani Pema continues, "Walking the walk means you're very genuine and down to earth. You take the teachings as good medicine for the things that are confusing to you and for the suffering of your life."

This weekend, there are 560 retreatants present, with an additional 1,200 people dialing in to the live stream from around the globe. As Ani Pema points out, most of us are attending because of our issues – our anger or addiction, our grief or loneliness. There are people here who are struggling with illness; there are people here who've lost their job. One woman is living with the memory of waking up to find her infant cold and blue. Someone else is trying to come to terms with her son's homelessness.

Every single one of us wants to hear something that is going to be of value in our life.

Over the weekend, Ani Pema will teach us about four qualities that are key to waking up. She feels they are critical for walking the walk and experiencing genuine transformation. Each of her four talks will focus on one of these qualities.

1. Stabilize Your Mind

When Ani Pema's late teacher, Chögyam Trungpa Rinpoche, was a child in Tibet, his primary teacher was a famous master named Jamgon Kongtrul Rinpoche. One day, Ani Pema tells us, Trungpa Rinpoche went to his teacher's room, where he found him sitting in front of a window with the soft morning light falling on his face. In his hands, Kongtrul Rinpoche held a metal object that was shaped like a peculiar comb and was the color of the silver bowls on shrines. It was something Trungpa Rinpoche had never seen before.

"In the West, they use this to eat," Kongtrul Rinpoche explained. "They poke it into meat and then they use it to lift the meat up and put it in their mouth. Someday, you're going to go where people eat with these things." At this point, Kongtrul Rinpoche smiled broadly at his prediction. "You might just find," he concluded, "that they're a lot more interested in staying asleep than in waking up."

Ani Pema believes that Kongtrul Rinpoche had a point: there is a lot of cultural support for unconsciousness in this land of forks. It's human nature to want to be distracted from uncomfortable, painful feelings such as boredom, restlessness, or bitterness. And now that we have such a multitude of ways to distract ourselves, from texting to television, it's even more challenging to be awake and fully present. Even when we turn off the ringer, our cellphone still vibrates and the pull to check it is almost irresistible.

In the face of all this temptation, stabilizing the mind is the basis for showing up for our own life.

"You could call it training or taming the mind to stay present," Ani Pema says, "but a more accurate way of describing it is strengthening the mind. That's because we are strengthening qualities we already have, rather than training in something that we have to bring in from the outside."

Throughout life, we have trained in distracting ourselves, so going unconscious feels like our natural MO. Our minds, however, have two essential qualities we can always draw on to help us wake up: being present and knowing what's happening, moment by moment. To strengthen these natural qualities of mind, we can use meditation.

This weekend, Buddhist teacher Elizabeth Mattis-Namgyel, author of *The Power of an Open Question*, is leading us in our meditation sessions. Having spent more than six years of her life in retreat, she's had ample practice. *Shamatha* meditation – calm abiding – is the technique she's teaching, and she breaks it down into three parts: body, breath, and mind.

"When you're meditating, the body should have some energy in it – it's not slumped over," Elizabeth says. "But, also, the body should be natural. Often, we think we have to 'assume the position,' and sometimes the position we assume is quite religious, kind of stiff.

"Meditation is really just learning to enjoy your experience, so you don't have to tense up. Don't make meditation a project like everything else. The word 'natural' is very important. Yesterday, I was walking around Omega, and it's so beautiful here. It feels like the last red leaf is about to drop, but it's still there. We appreciate nature because it's so uncontrived and unselfconscious. Bring that to mind and know that the body itself has its own intelligence."

Next, we have the breath, Elizabeth continues. "We breathe in. There's this natural pause, and then the outbreath. There's another pause. Then again, breathing in." But don't imagine that just because we're focusing on our breath that everything else will go blank and our senses will close down. The breath is simply what we keep bringing the mind back to.

"The mind will get lost because it's habituated to escaping the present moment," Elizabeth explains. "So when you start getting lost in the activity of the mind, or when you see yourself bracing against experience in some way, be joyful because you've noticed! Don't be hard on yourself. You get lost and you keep coming back – this is what's supposed to happen."

According to Elizabeth, the key to shamatha practice is to approach it with a bit of fierceness – not aggressive fierceness, but the fierceness of true commitment. Shamatha is a very basic practice, she says. Don't, however, underestimate it. It's extremely powerful.

Elizabeth shares with us the story of a friend of hers who suffered abuse as a child. This woman ended up living on the streets and selling drugs to support her own habit. Then she got arrested and was sent to a high-security prison, where she got put into solitary confinement for a year and a half.

One day, she was outside her cell for a brief break when she happened to meet a cook who worked in the prison kitchen. They talked for just a moment, but in that time, he told her that if she didn't learn to train her mind, she would go crazy in solitary confinement.

"I don't know how to meditate," the prisoner told the cook. "I only know how to count and pace." That's fine, he counseled. Just focus on that. And so, she did. For a year and half, she could only walk seven steps in each direction, but counting and pacing was her calm abiding meditation. Today, says Elizabeth, "She's organized and beautiful and caring and has a good relationship to her world."

"In the Buddhist tradition," Elizabeth explains, "we say that the untamed mind is like a limbless blind person trying to ride a wild horse. There's not much choice in just letting that situation continue. You create choice by reining in the mind."

2. Make Friends with Yourself

One of Pema Chödrön's students wrote her a letter. "You talk about gentleness all the time," he began, "but secretly, I always thought that gentleness was for girls." When Ani Pema recounts this story, the retreatants – predominantly female – laugh. Unsurprisingly, once this student tried being gentle with himself, he had a change of heart. In the face of things he found embarrassing or humiliating, he realized that it takes a lot of courage to be gentle.

Ani Pema points out that practicing meditation can actually ramp up our habitual self-denigration. This is because, in the process of stabilizing the mind, we become more aware of traits in ourselves that we don't like, whether it's cruelty, cynicism, or selfishness. Then we need to look deeper, with even more clarity. When we examine our addictions, for example, we need to be able to see the sadness that's behind having another drink, the loneliness behind another joint.

This brings us to unconditional friendship with ourselves, the second quality that Ani Pema teaches is critical for waking up. As she explains it, "When you have a true friend, you stick together year after year, but you don't put your friend up on a pedestal and think that they're perfect. You two have had fights. You've seen them be really petty, you've seen them mean, and they've also seen you in all different states of mind. Yet you remain friends, and there's even something about the fact that you know each other so well and still love each other that strengthens the friendship. Your friendship is based on knowing each other fully and still loving each other."

Unconditional friendship with yourself has the same flavor as the deep friendships you have with others. You know yourself but you're kind to yourself. You even love yourself when you think you've blown it once again. In fact, Ani Pema teaches, it is only through unconditional friendship with yourself that your issues will budge. Repressing your tendencies, shaming yourself, calling yourself bad – these will never help you realize transformation.

Keep in mind that the transformation Ani Pema is talking about is not going from being a bad person to being a good person. It is a process of getting smarter about what helps and what hurts; what de-escalates suffering and escalates it; what increases happiness and what obscures it. It is about loving yourself so much that you don't want to make yourself suffer anymore.

Ani Pema wraps up her Saturday morning talk by taking questions. One woman who comes up to the mic says she's been on the spiritual path for a while, yet it doesn't seem to be helping her. Ani Pema – as she always does – fully engages with the questioner.

"Do you have a regular meditation practice?" she asks.

"Yes."

"And how does that feel these days?"

"It feels hurried."

"Hurried?"

"I have a child with disabilities, so meditation has to be fit in. I can't just decide to go sit down. It has to be set up."

"I get it," Ani Pema says slowly. "So, okay, that's how it is currently – uncomfortable, hurried. Things as they are." Then she comes back to what we've been talking about this morning: unconditional friendship. Ani Pema's advice is this: don't reject what you see in yourself; embrace it instead. Feeling Hurried Buddha, Feeling Cut Off from Nature Buddha, Feeling No Compassion Buddha – recognize the buddha in each feeling.

3. Be Free from Fixed Mind

Nestled in the Hudson River Valley, Omega Institute is like camp for spiritually minded adults. In the mornings, I attend a yoga or tai chi class before the sun comes up. In the evenings, I go to the Ram Dass Library and read on a window seat lined with cushions patterned with elephants. Other retreatants choose the sauna or the sanctuary, the basketball or tennis courts, the lively café or the liquid-glass lake. And the food is good, too – healthy dishes such as black beans over rice, spiced with salsa verde and topped with dollops of sour cream and sprinkles of cheese.

It's Saturday afternoon and, having indulged too much at lunch, I'm in a cozy stupor when Ani Pema asks us all to stand up. We're going to do an exercise. Inhaling, we're going to raise our hands high in the air. Then exhaling with a "hah," we're going to quickly bring our arms down and slap our palms against our thighs. Simple enough, but the result is surprising. Although those are *my* hands making contact with *my* thighs, the jolt is unexpected. Suddenly, if just for the briefest of moments, I feel lucid, totally fresh. This, says Ani Pema, is an experience of being free from fixed mind.

Fixed mind is stuck, inflexible. It's a mind that closes down, that is living with blinders on. Though it's a common state in everyday life, fixed mind is particularly easy to spot in the realm of politics.

"Say you're an environmentalist," Ani Pema tells us. "What you're working for is really important, but when fixed mind comes in, the other side is the enemy. You become prejudiced and closed, and this makes you less effective as an activist."

On the spiritual path, being free from fixed mind is the third necessary quality for waking up. Even if we aren't practitioners, life itself gives us endless opportunities to experience this freedom. These, for instance, are all things that have stopped my mind: loud, jolting noises; intense beauty, such as the sudden glimpse of an enormous orange moon; and surrealist art, such as Salvador Dali's telephone with a lobster inexplicably perched on top.

"The experience of being free of fixed mind often happens because of trauma or crisis," Ani Pema says. A sudden death or tragedy takes place, and on a dime we see that things are not the way we usually perceive them. Ani Pema tells the story of one woman who, on September 11, 2001, experienced a profound gap in just this way. Distracted and rushed, she was heading to work with her arms full of papers for a presentation she was about to give. Then she came up out of the subway and saw the destruction. The air was filled with papers like the ones she was holding – all the paperwork that had been filling up drawers in offices like hers. Her mind stopped.

When Ani Pema first started practicing meditation, she felt poverty-stricken because everyone in her circle was always talking about "the gap." That's the open awareness that's revealed when we're free from fixed mind, but she never experienced it and whenever she admitted this to someone, they'd smile smugly. "You will," they'd say.

As she understood it, the gap was supposed to be something experienced in meditation, yet, she says, "What was happening with me was pretty much *yak-yak-yak*, intermingled with strong reactivity and emotional responses. But then I was in the meditation hall for a month. It was summer and there was this continual hum of the air conditioner. It never stopped, so after a while you didn't hear it anymore. I was sitting there one day and somebody turned the air conditioner off. That was it! Gap!"

This simple experience gave Ani Pema a reference point for being free from fixed mind. It shifted her meditation practice and her life. "I'd be having a conversation with someone," she explains. "I'd be getting all heated up and I would begin to have this sense of my mouth and my mind going *yak-yak-yak*. Then I got the hang of how I could just drop it. I could give myself a break and experience being free from fixed mind. Of course, the mind starts up again, just the way the air conditioner did. But once you've had the experience of this gap, or pause, you begin to notice that it happens a lot automatically."

A practitioner's work is noticing the gaps and appreciating them. In every action, every sound, every sight and smell, there can be some space, and in it there is wonder or awe at every – supposedly – mundane turn. "The potential of your human life is so enormous and so vast," says Ani Pema.

At the end of her talk everyone bows, and I concentrate on letting the gesture be a doorway – a simple thing that can expand. There is the delicate wonder of my fingers curled lightly around my thighs and the solemn wonder of my back folding softly forward. There's the awe of again sitting up straight and the awe of standing up and the awe of streaming toward the door with the other retreatants.

Outside, the sunlight is beginning to weaken into pale pink as I find the trailhead near the meditation hall. Until dinner, I listen to the wonder of my sneakers crunching and rustling while I walk through fallen oak leaves.

4. Take Care of Each Other

My fellow retreatants Lelia Calder and Cynthia Ronar are sharing a cabin, and I pop by to ask them about their experience with Pema Chödrön's teachings. Lelia, a resident of Pennsylvania, has been a dedicated student since the mid '90s. Cynthia, from Ohio, has never before been to a retreat with Ani Pema but has been reading her books for five years.

When I ask Lelia for an example of how Pema Chödrön's teachings have helped her in life, she laughs. "There have been so many! I wish I could think of one that is very dramatic but a lot of the time, they're just so simple. We make things very complicated, but I think one of the things about dharma is that it really is simple. When things get simple, they seem like no big deal. Yet it is a big deal to be simple and direct and uncomplicated – to not make a big problem out of your life."

Cynthia says the teachings strike a chord because she can relate to Pema Chödrön's life experiences. Ani Pema frequently talks about how it was her second divorce that took her to her edge and brought her to the Buddhist path; Cynthia also endured a painful separation.

"There were times when I literally felt, I don't know what to do," says Cynthia. "I don't know how to get off the floor right now. But because of Pema's teachings, I learned that I could just be there. It was great to have someone say, 'Yeah, you're on the floor! I've been on the floor, too. And you can stay there. Just stop the story line. If you stop it for two seconds, you've moved forward.'"

Meredith Monk is a renowned composer and performer who is a longtime student of Pema Chödrön's. When I interview her under the umbrella of a tree, she tells me how Ani Pema helped her gain a wider perspective after her partner's death.

"When we're in very painful circumstances," Meredith explains, "there's a way we can see that those circumstances are part of the big flow of life. At the same moment that you're having that pain, there are millions of other people who are having that same kind of pain. There are millions of other people sitting in a hospital waiting room. There are millions of people who are dealing with grief."

During her last talk of the weekend, Ani Pema states: "When you feel bad, let it be your link to others' suffering. When you feel good, let it be your link with others' joy." This understanding that our sorrows and joys are not separate from the sorrows and joys of others is a key to the fourth and final quality that is critical for waking up: taking care of one another.

Sea anemones are open and soft, but if you put your finger anywhere near them, they close. This, says Ani Pema, is what we're like. We can't stand to see our flaws or failings; we can't stand our feelings of boredom, disappointment, or fear; we can't stand to witness the suffering on the evening news or in the face of the homeless person on the corner. And so, we shut down.

"That's a kind of sanity," Ani Pema posits. "Your body and mind intuitively know what's enough. But in your heart, you have this strong aspiration that before you die – and hopefully even by next week – that you'll become more capable of being open to other people and yourself. The attitude is one step at a time – four baby steps forward, two baby steps back. You can just allow it to be like that. Trust that you have to go at your own speed."

Habitually, we allow our difficult emotions and experiences to isolate us from others. We feel alone in our depression or desperation or sadness. But when we use these to link us to everyone else in the world who's suffering in the same way, we find that we are not alone, and we discover a deep well of compassion for others.

I take a long look around at my neighboring retreatants. Ani Pema, wrapping up the last talk of the weekend, is seated at the front with her glass of water and a flower arrangement. Flanking me, there is a middle-aged woman in a butterfly blouse and hoop earrings and a young woman in a hoodie and thumb ring. In front of me there is a man with a wisp of ponytail. Together, five hundred-plus voices chant these four ancient lines from the Buddhist sage Shantideva:

> *And now as long as space endures,*
> *As long as there are beings to be found,*
> *May I continue likewise to remain*
> *To drive away the sorrows of the world.*

Steel, Roses, & Slave Ships

Miya Ando, Sanford Biggers, and Chrysanne Stathacos – Three Artists Drawing on Buddhist Wisdom

Miya Ando, Steel Horizons

Miya Ando is wearing head-to-toe black, except for the pearly Buddhist prayer beads around her wrist. But greeting me at the door of her Brooklyn studio, what she wants to show me is pure, vibrant color: the robes she inherited from her grandfather. Ando's grandfather was the head priest of a small Buddhist temple in Okayama, Japan, where she spent half her childhood. She remembers clearly the sound of chanting through the paper-thin walls and seeing her grandfather dressed in these robes, which she is now carefully unwrapping. They're made of almost luminescent purple and orange damask and still smell faintly of temple incense.

Purple is an unusual color for Nichiren Buddhist robes, Ando tells me, because it's reserved for those who have been priests for fifty years or more. It is this purple and the contrast-ing orange that's got her thinking about the impact of color and how she can incorporate it into her art.

This is a departure from the gray scale that has long been Ando's focus. She's a descendant of the celebrated samurai sword maker Ando Yoshiro Masakatsu, and following in his footsteps, her principal material is steel. She has made whimsical steel sculptures of traditional Japanese shoes, steel kimonos embla-zoned with her Japanese family's crest of wisteria, and even a steel skateboard. But over the years her chief passion has been creating two-dimensional steel panels. They are, effectively, steel

canvases on which she "paints" by sanding, grinding, and applying heat and patinas. Look at these panels in one state of mind
and they are abstract fields of nothingness. Look at them again
and they are vast vistas and distant horizons. "I am putting forth
imagery that is universal," explains Ando. "Anyone can look at a
rectilinear form that is bisected and say horizon – land and sky, or
sea and sky. That is a natural division of space to any human. It's
a universal language and, I hope, a comforting language."

Wanting her art to speak to everyone is important to Ando
because her personal experience straddles East and West. Her
mother is Japanese and her father is a first-generation Jewish-
Russian American. Growing up, she split her time between her
family's temple in Japan and living off the grid on twenty-five
acres of redwoods in California. "I very much feel American," she
says, "but I'm also greatly inspired by my Buddhist background
and living in Japan."

The Buddhist concept Ando keeps coming back to in her
work is impermanence. There's sadness in it for her, but also
beauty. Ephemerality is what connects everything and everyone, she says. Steel holds up bridges and buildings and conjures
up a sense of permanence. Yet even steel, one of the strongest
substances we have on Earth, will at some point dissolve. This
industrial metal reminds us of its vulnerability by reflecting the
fleetingness of light and absorbing shifting color.

Sparked by her grandfather's robes, soothingly colored
squares of steel canvas are now hanging on Ando's studio walls,
and near the door there's a majestic steel kimono with shades of
pink and red on the sleeves and skirt. She places in my hands a
cube of solid aluminum, tinted lilac. "Monochrome color meditations" is how Ando describes her new steel panels in blue, gold,
green, and purple, as well as the circular "mandalas" that she
makes from a variety of metals.

Not only do her color meditations invite the viewer to find
stillness, the process by which Ando creates them – applying one
layer of pigment each day – is also meditative. She has always

approached her studio work as a contemplative practice. As soon as Ando enters her studio, she does sitting meditation. Then, following her family's Nichiren tradition, she chants and prays. After that, mindful of her actions and her breath, she works on her art, fully absorbed in each task. She calls the way she works "walking meditation" but explains that it's more meditation of movement that is based on traditional walking meditation.

Ando doesn't have a particular temple that she attends in the U.S. because, as she sees it, her family's temple is something she carries within her. "I'm not a Buddhist who feels the need for a certain cushion or 100 percent silence," she says. "In my upbringing, I learned that practice – being conscious, being mindful – is like brushing your teeth. It's an everyday thing."

Sanford Biggers, B-bodhisattva

The disk of glass is seven feet wide and hand etched with an image of a lotus. Crisp, clean, and modern, it's a calming and pretty piece – until you get close enough to see the details. Each lotus petal is the cross section of a slave ship, based on actual eighteenth-century diagrams depicting the most efficient means of storing human cargo. The people are packed shoulder to shoulder. The lotus is a Buddhist symbol of transformation. For artist Sanford Biggers, making a lotus out of slave ships was a way of transcending a painful history.

Biggers does not consider himself a Buddhist but he is strongly influenced by Buddhism. Buddhist teachings on the middle way were what first captured his attention because, as he sees it, they relate to growing up black in America and learning to cope with both subtle and overt racism. For Biggers, living the middle way means not letting things that are good or bad take him too far away from being centered.

In Biggers' haunting installation *Blossom*, he explores the experience of African Americans. This large-scale piece can be viewed as a tree growing out of a piano or a piano hanging out of a tree. The instrument is playing Biggers' version of "Strange Fruit," a song made famous by Billie Holiday. It is about lynching. "The tree sees the good and the bad," Biggers says. "The tree sees everything." Trees have indeed been used for lynching, but it was also under a tree that Siddhartha obtained enlightenment. The tree transcends dualities.

In 2004, Biggers spent four months in Japan doing an artist residency and practicing meditation at a Soto Zen temple. To prepare for the residency, he went to various shops in his Harlem neighborhood and bought hip-hop jewelry. Then, once in Tokyo, he had the collection melted down and shaped into singing bowls, which were polished and engraved with the words Hip Hop Ni Sasagu, meaning "Farewell to Hip-hop."

"Hip-hop had gone from a rebel type of music that often had political and poignant messages to something that's all about bling and money," says Biggers. "In that respect, I thought the spirit of hip-hop had died."

As a memorial, Biggers performed a bell ceremony at the Zen temple. He was joined by the head monk and fifteen other participants, none of whom were professional musicians. Each participant was invited to strike their assigned singing bowl whenever they felt it was appropriate. By improvising in this way, different aesthetics came into play and all participants were able to take part without having to train or read notation.

Returning to the United States, Biggers – a former b-boy – began creating dance floors that he calls his B-bodhisattva series. They were made from surplus rubber tiles that he got from an old factory in Chicago – the kind of tiles that used to be on high school floors in the '60s and '70s. They had a particular color saturation that reminded him of Buddhist mandalas, so he hand-cut the tiles and arranged them into mandalas of his own design. Biggers then took the mandalas/dance floors to breakdancing competitions, where he'd put a video camera above the floor and record dancers as the circles of their movements echoed the circular gestures of the floor itself. He would later show these videos and the floors – with all their scuff marks – at museums. He'd invite b-boys to the openings, and for a few hours each week the floors would usually be available for the public to dance on. The idea, he says, was that a floor would "collect more and more scuff marks as people danced on it. It would be like a patchwork quilt made by many different people – a dance floor made by different dancers."

"Art exists, but it doesn't really complete itself until the viewer has some interaction with it," Biggers says. "This is the same exchange as playing in a band. As an artist, all I do is propose something visually. The viewer has to do a bit of work to make the piece complete."

Chrysanne Stathacos, Impermanence of the Beautiful

Chrysanne Stathacos looked over the fence and saw a man in yellow and maroon robes jumping up and down in her friend's yard. It was the spring of 1975 in Vancouver, and this was the first Tibetan lama she had ever seen. Later that day, the lama was going to give a public teaching, and Stathacos piled into the car with her friend, the lama, and the lama's translator. When they stopped at a red light, however, Stathacos suddenly bolted from the car. "It's not time for me to do this yet," she blurted out.

Now Stathacos speculates that she wasn't ready to go with the lama in 1975 because her focus was so much on art that she had nothing to spare for spiritual life. She was only five years old when she announced to her mother that she was an artist and "that was that," she says.

Stathacos – born in 1951 in Buffalo, New York – was raised Greek Orthodox. But, she asserts, "I was precocious in Sunday school. I never understood why there wasn't a female in the Trinity and I would always ask, 'Where's Mary?' At that time women couldn't go behind a certain point in the altar, so I would ask, 'Well, why is Mrs. Pappas allowed there to clean?'"

It wasn't until the late 1990s that Stathacos finally connected with a spiritual female voice. She was traveling in India when a friend invited her to a talk by Jetsunma Tenzin Palmo, a Western Buddhist nun who'd been in retreat in a Himalayan cave for twelve years. In the middle of the talk, Tenzin Palmo asked the audience, "Do you understand?" And Stathacos thought: Oh, God, I understand that I don't understand, and now I have to get a teacher.

Today Stathacos is a student of Gehlek Rinpoche and a founding director of Dongyu Gatsal Ling Initiatives. It's an organization dedicated to reclaiming the lost traditions of Tibetan women practitioners by supporting nunneries in India and Tibet. Stathacos' Buddhist practice also informs her art. This can be seen most clearly in her *Rose Mandalas*, one of which she made for the Dalai Lama when he attended the 2006 conference Law, Buddhism, and Social Change at the University of Buffalo.

The Rose Mandalas range from ten to sixty feet in diameter, and Stathacos makes them by plucking apart roses and circling the petals around mirrors. When the mandalas are fresh, they're florally fragrant. Then over time the petals shrivel. Finally, the mandalas are dismantled in a ritual performance; they're swept up or blown away with human breath.

In Tenzin Palmo's words, "*The Rose Mandalas* symbolize the gradual unfolding of our innate spiritual potential. Conversely, these mandalas remind us of the inherent impermanence of even the beautiful."

Ritual is at the heart of much of Stathacos' creative output, particularly the ritual of wish-making. In 2001, Stathacos visited rock gardens in Japan and at one temple in Kyoto, the monks showed her some large stones covered with snow. They said that taken together these stones were in the form of the Buddha reclining. This inspired Stathacos to create *Refuge, a Wish Garden*, an interactive public artwork that she has presented on both German and American soil.

Refuge, a Wish Garden comprises a circle of sand with a large tree in the center. Around the tree there are eight wooden benches, painted eight different colors, and between the benches there are baskets filled with strips of fabric, rocks, sticks, and flowers. The public is invited to sit and engage in quiet contemplation. Then they can make a wish and take an action – to tie a piece of fabric to the tree, place a rock or flower, or use a stick to draw in the sand. Stathacos is fascinated by the fact that people across the globe tend to make wishes on natural objects, such as when they see a shooting star or when they toss a coin into a body of water. More than that, she's fascinated by wishes themselves and has collected them from the public worldwide, including from homeless youth.

"When you give people the opportunity to write down their wishes," Stathacos says, "you might think most of them would say they want something material." But, in fact, people frequently think beyond themselves. They think compassionately. Here is one that has touched her: "I wish that bullets would turn to roses and hatred to friendship."

Wisdom of the Rebels

A Q&A with Tom Robbins

A merican novelist Tom Robbins has a well-deserved cult
following, not just of gray-haired hippies but also fresh-
faced students, backpackers in Banana Republics, and others.
Take *Jitterbug Perfume*, the first book by Robbins that I was lucky
enough to stumble across at the local library – how can one not
be smitten by it? It's a book that begins with beets – "the most
intense of vegetables" – and then dives into heady perfume, a
good poke at a few of the world's major religions, and a host
of zany characters, including a 1,000-year-old janitor. Clearly
Robbins owes some inspiration to psychedelics, but this word-
slinger, as he calls himself, also owes something to Eastern
philosophy. His heroes are the Zen rebels, Sufi saints, and wild
yogis of the "crazy wisdom" tradition, as he interprets it. Like
them, Tom Robbins cuts through self-serious, conventional mind
with humor, insight, and a little bit of weirdness.

How would you define crazy wisdom?

The quick and easy answer is that crazy wisdom is the de-
liberate opposite of conventional wisdom. Like most quick and
easy answers, however, that one isn't really satisfying.

For want of a precise definition, we might consider that
crazy wisdom is a philosophical worldview that recommends
swimming against the tide, cheerfully seizing the short end of
the stick, embracing insecurity, honoring paradox, courting the
unexpected, celebrating the unfamiliar, shunning each and every
orthodoxy, volunteering for those tasks nobody else wants or
dares to do, and perhaps above all else, breaking taboos in order

to destroy their power. It's the wisdom of those who turn the tables on despair by lampooning it, and who neither seek authority nor submit to it.

What's the point of all this? To enlarge the soul, light up the brain, and liberate the spirit. Crazy wisdom is both transformative and transcendent.

You seem to be particularly partial to Zen Buddhism. Is it Zen's version of crazy wisdom that appeals to you, or are there other elements that draw you to it?

The branch of Zen Buddhism that has long interested me is Rinzai, the sect that eschews the mind-quieting practice of meditation in favor of the mind-blowing activity of wrestling with koans. Koans, of course, are those carefully crafted riddles that can never be solved by means of anything remotely resembling deductive logic.

On a purely intellectual level, attempting to solve koans is a perfect manifestation of crazy wisdom at work. It's important to emphasize, however, that, unlike Zen, crazy wisdom is not a practice, it's an *attitude* (an attitude I seem to have had since birth).

In general, I'm attracted to Zen's focus on absolute freedom and all-embracing oneness, its reverence for nature, and its respect for humor. When Zen or tantric masters visit North America, they're often astonished by how earnest, how overly serious, Westerners are about their spiritual practice. They'll go to a zendo in Minnesota, for example, and wonder aloud why nobody there is laughing. This led Chögyam Trungpa, in a lovely expression of crazy wisdom, to squirt righteously zealous meditators with a water pistol.

To be uptight about one's Zen practice, to become attached to it, is to miss the whole point of it; one might as well hook up with one of the fear-based, authoritarian, guilt-and-redemption religions.

Can you give me some examples of crazy wisdom that interest you?

I'm a word-slinger not a scholar, I have a monkey mind not a monk mind, but I think you can trust me when I report that just as Zen evolved in China from a co-mingling of Buddhism and Taoism, there occurred in Tibet a dynamic meeting between Buddhism and Bön, the ancient Tibetan shamanic religion. The Buddhist masters who had infiltrated Tibet (around the eighth century) were eccentric *mahasiddhas* out of the tantric lineage in India, and the Bön shamans, having a natural affinity, took to their crazy-wisdom ways like Homer Simpson to donuts, maybe even improving (if "improving" is the right word) on their radical approach to ultimate awareness.

The Tibetan *siddhas* soon acquired a reputation as the wildest of spiritual outlaws. Siddhas slept naked in the snow, hung out in graveyards, nibbled on dung, drank wine from skulls, publicly engaged in kinky sex, and missed no opportunity to ridicule dogma. Believing in the possibility of instant karma, they employed shock tactics to jolt people into spontaneous enlightenment.

When a latter-day Japanese roshi would define buddhahood as "dried shit on a stick," or answer the question, "What do you do when you meet your master coming through the woods?" by advising, "Hit him over the head with a stick," you know they'd been infected with the virus of crazy wisdom.

Whether it sprang up independently in Persia and Turkey or was carried there by travelers along the Silk Road, I haven't a clue, but crazy wisdom permeates Sufism. One of my favorite Sufi stories concerns a man who, feeling in need of spiritual guidance, petitions for an audience with a renowned master. After a long wait, the request is granted, but the man is allowed to ask only one question. He asks, "What is God really like?"

The master answers, "God? God is a carrot. Ha ha ha ha ha!"

Feeling mocked and insulted, the man goes away in a snit. Later, suspecting that he must have misunderstood something, he requests a second interview, and after several years it, too, is granted. "What did you mean," the fellow asks, "when you said God is a carrot?"

The master looks at him in amazement. "A carrot?" he bellows. "God is not a carrot! God is a radish!" And again he laughs uproariously.

Turned away, the fellow broods over this outlandishness for many months. Then, one day, it dawns on him that the master was saying that God is beyond definition and can never be described, that anything we might say is God is automatically not God. At that moment, the man was powerfully awakened.

Examples of crazy wisdom also abound in the modern West, ranging from Joris Karl Huysmans sewing his eyelids shut because he believed that at age thirty, he'd already seen so much it would take him the rest of his life to process it all, to Muhammad Ali dancing in his undershorts at the Houston Induction Center after committing a felony by refusing to be conscripted into the army.

Unfortunately, however, crazy wisdom in the West is almost always devoid of a spiritual dimension.

What influences or happenings in your life first prompted you to have a spiritual attitude?

When I left home at age seventeen, I quit attending church because church had been providing me with nothing beyond an anesthetic numbing of the backside and the brain. By my mid-twenties, I'd completely rejected my Southern Baptist faith on the grounds that it was a bastion of fascist-tinged hypocrisy, based on misinterpretation of Levantine myth and watered-down compromises of the teachings of Jesus. Around that time, I began peeking into Asian systems of liberation, but it wasn't until my early thirties that I was literally propelled into the spiritual zone by the oceanic blast of psychedelic drugs.

Traditionalists won't like hearing this, but the fact is, tens of thousands of Westerners became receptive to and enamored of Buddhist and Hindu teachings as a direct result of LSD.

Over time you have changed your mind about whether or not Americans can thoroughly and successfully adopt Asian philosophies such as Buddhism or Taoism. What is your opinion now?

There are numerous paths to enlightenment. In Asia, the paths have been worn smooth by millions of experienced feet. The Western seeker, while he or she may have ready access to guides, maps, and road signs imported from Asia, must nevertheless stumble along overgrown, unfamiliar trails pitted with potholes and patrolled by our indigenous cultural wolves.

Americans may hold Buddhist ideals in our hearts and minds, but they're not yet in our genes. That takes time. Meanwhile, Asians are becoming increasingly Americanized. Who knows where this exchange will lead?

In your first novel, Another Roadside Attraction, *your character Marx Marvelous contemplates what religion would take Christianity's place if Christianity were suddenly to disappear. Can you describe the faith that you think might develop in such a situation?*

Suppose that from the environmentalist movement there should spring a revival of mystical nature worship, and suppose that this new nature religion should receive an infusion of crazy wisdom sufficient to keep it honest and amusing, free from any trace of dogma. Wouldn't that be the wildcat's meow?

In real life, the religious right has gained a lot of power in the U.S. over the past number of years. What are your predictions regarding how this situation will develop in the years to come?

There may seem to be a whiff of paranoid fantasy about it, but it's really not unreasonable to suggest that the Christian right presents by far the greatest threat to human existence in all of history.

I have a friend, a high-ranking officer in Naval Intelligence, who assures me that the U.S. intelligence services, military and civilian, are becoming packed with evangelical Christians. Congress and the White House are known to be heavily influenced by evangelicals, their doctrine, their votes, and their money. The danger they present is that they desperately want widespread war in the Middle East, they hunger for the fire and blood of Armageddon, thinking that it will force Jesus to come back and remove the "righteous" from this earthly existence that confuses and disgusts them.

U.S. foreign policy is now based on the apocalyptic Book of Revelation, which is to say, based on the ravings of a long-dead misogynistic madman. When he lived in Ephesus, the first thing the Apostle John saw every morning upon awakening was the gigantic statue of Artemis, with her multitude of naked breasts, and she made him crazy (though hardly wise). The Book of Revelation is the result. What sort of hallucinations do you think ol' John might have suffered had he run into Britney Spears?

As sentient beings, as a part of the One, the fundamentalist spawn of John deserve our compassion, but because they increasingly imperil all life on the planet, they must also be vigorously opposed.

Your book Still Life with Woodpecker *explores how to make love stay. How would you define love?*

Love is a carrot. No, no, it's a radish. Listen, better brains than mine have skidded off the road in pursuit of that elusive subject. I can say this much with confidence: genuine love, while it lasts, is a transformative emotional state that makes of the loved one an irreplaceable being. There's something magical, magnificent, and very sweet about that.

Since writing Still Life with Woodpecker, *have you learned anything new about how to make love stay?*

Well, I've learned that in asking how we can make love stay, I posed the wrong question. Romantic love moves around. That's what it does. Indifferent to misguided human cravings for permanence and certainty, it stages its glorious show, then folds its tent and leaves town. Or, at least, it stops buttering the popcorn. Perhaps it's both insulting and injurious to romance to try to hold on to it.

Ah, but there's another kind of love that does stay – and most Buddhists are familiar with it. When you "fall" into universal love, you're "in" love all the time, external events notwithstanding; you live and breathe in love. Even then, should your romantic partner decamp, you might feel sad or even angry for a while, but you won't sit up night after night swilling tequila and listening to heartbreak music.

It should be noted that there are relationships between mature, grounded, personally evolved individuals (people whole enough not to cling or be needy) that do last, and sometimes manage to embody both the romantic *and* the spiritual.

In your book Wild Ducks Flying Backward, *you say that the word "spiritual" has become highly suspect. Why do you say that? How and why did the word degenerate?*

When a blue-collar, average Joe hears the word "spiritual," he'll frequently hee-haw and spit. It sounds sissy, elitist, and heretical to him, a threat to his masculinity and a contamination of the patriotic and religious detergents with which his brain has been thoroughly washed. When cool urban cynics hear the word, they sneer. It's an affront to their existential hipness.

For many others, it's a reminder of the legions of charlatans, frauds, and self-deluded dilettantes who are making money by hawking various brands of "spiritual" guidance. Then, too, there are the innocent airheads who go about broadcasting embarrassing streams of woo-woo in their everyday lives (and who are frequently the victims of the con-artist gurus).

These folks – some greedy, some ignorant, some just sweetly naïve – have all contributed to the aura of suspicion that surrounds the word "spiritual" in contemporary American society. That's indeed unfortunate, because spirituality, when pure, connects us to the godhead with infinitely more efficacy and grace than does religiosity.

What is the most spiritual place you have ever visited?

An uninhabited savannah deep in Africa, a hundred miles from any artificial light, where, while lions coughed and night birds sang, I gazed at a dozen wheeling constellations and millions of ancient sparkling stars.

If it were true, after all, that humans were made in the image of God, what exactly do you think God would look like?

God is a carrot. Wait a second, that's not right. God is a radish!

Buddha's Birds

From the Swan Siddhartha Nursed as a Boy to the Fantastical Garuda

In my freshman year of college, my religious studies class was at the sleepy hour of two o'clock, and to make matters worse the professor was hypnotically soft-spoken and wore tired shades of brown. So, on the day that he slowly enumerated the four noble truths on the board, I failed to experience the flash of insight, which many Buddhist converts talk about; the only thing I felt was my heavy eyelids.

Then I glimpsed movement.

I was sitting by the window – sunlight pouring in – and a dark, glossy bird I didn't have a name for was on the stone windowsill outside. If it weren't for the glass, I could have touched it – I was that close to its iridescent purple and green sheen, blunt tail, and yellow bill. Watching the bird tilting its head as it looked at me with alert, shiny eyes, I was suddenly wholly focused.

I'd never before paid much attention to birds, but for me this particular one was what Zen master Thich Nhat Hanh calls "a bell of mindfulness." The bird woke me up to the present moment.

It was inevitable: I became both a Buddhist and a birdwatcher.

For me, birding is a form of meditation – it's just watching, just listening. I appreciate how birding encourages equanimity, how it helps me rest in ambiguity and uncertainty. In the field, I get a glimpse of small, brown wings disappearing through the branches of an oak. Then I look through my bird books and see page after page of almost indistinguishable little brown birds with their subtle markings and minor differences. Did the bird I see have yellow or tan legs? Was its beak straight or did it curve? I can't positively identify the bird and I have to find some peace with that.

It's easy to find symbolism in birds – in the way they take flight, in the way they preen and nest and sing. Poets have long made wordy use of their wings, while mystics have revered them. In Buddhism, birds are used to teach ethics and concepts. They are metaphors for our muddled, unskillful selves, and also represent our best, no-self selves. Buddhist bird lore goes all the way back to the beginning, or so the story goes.

Siddhartha and the Swan

One day, when the future Buddha, Siddhartha, was just a child, he and his cousin Devadatta went walking in the forest. Devadatta was an avid hunter, never without his bow and a sheaf of arrows, so when a wedge of swans passed through the sky, he aimed at the leading bird and pierced its wing. As the swan fell heavily to the ground both boys ran to it, but it was Siddhartha who arrived first. He cradled the injured creature in his arms and whispered comfort into its curved, milky neck. Then he extracted the shaft of the arrow and rubbed the wound with a cool and soothing herb.

Eventually, Devadatta caught up to Siddhartha and demanded he hand over the swan, but Siddhartha refused. When Devadatta persisted, Siddhartha suggested that they bring the matter to the king, and so in front of the whole court Devadatta and Siddhartha each presented their side of the argument. They were both so persuasive that the court was divided; some people thought that the swan belonged to Devadatta because he shot it, while others believed that it was Siddhartha's for nursing it.

Suddenly, an elderly man appeared and the king asked him his opinion. "The prized possession of every creature is its life," the elder stated. "As such, a creature belongs to whoever protects it, not to the one who attempts to take its life away."

Seeing the wisdom in this, the court awarded Siddhartha the swan. He sheltered it until it was fully healed, and then set it free.

The Golden Goose

The Buddha often told his followers stories about his previous lives to teach them ethical lessons. According to one story, he was once a man who died and was reborn as a golden goose. He still remembered his old family and felt a pang thinking of how, since his death, they were just barely scraping by. So he went to them and at their feet he released one of his valuable feathers. "I'll always provide for you," the goose promised. Then each day after that he gave the family another feather until they had enough gold to buy soft beds and rich foods.

But his former wife grew greedy, and one day she lured the goose close to her with sweet words. Then she grabbed him, pinned his beating wings between her chest and the crook of her arm, and plucked all of his resplendent feathers. Now, the goose couldn't fly away, so his wife threw him into a barrel, fed him skinny scraps of food, and waited for his feathers to grow back. But when they did, she was disappointed: instead of the golden glint she was hoping for, the new feathers were as white as icy silence.

The Rooster of Attachment

Buddhist teachings place a bird at the very center of the wheel of life, the *bhavacakra*. At root, Buddhism is about how we can find true liberation from the suffering of *samsara*, the wheel of cyclic existence. The bhavacakra, which some say the Buddha himself created as a teaching tool, is both a diagram to help us see why we're stuck in samsara and a map to help us find freedom from it.

At the hub of the wheel of life there are three animals: a bird, a pig, and a snake. In English we refer to this bird as a rooster or cock, but Tibetan teacher Ringu Tulku says that it's actually an Asian species, one that is obsessively attached to its mate. The bird, therefore, represents desire, clinging, or attachment, while the snake symbolizes aggression or aversion and the pig sym-bolizes ignorance or indifference. Together, these three animals represent the three poisons – passion, aggression, and ignorance – that drive the wheel of samsara.

If you look around, you may notice that the whole well of our world is poisoned. From the spider crawling on your shin to the climate crisis to a box of chocolates with creamy centers – everything in our unenlightened lives always comes down to "I want it," "I don't want it," or "I don't care about it." It's through this attachment, aversion, or indifference that karma or action arises, which in turn gives rise to suffering. In short, the three poisons are the venomous fuel that drives samsara.

Look again at the animals in the center of the wheel. Fre-quently, the bird and snake are depicted coming out of the pig's mouth, while at the same time they are clenching his tail. This hints at how the poisons bleed into each other: desire and aver-sion not only stem from ignorance, they also feed it.

As Roshi Bernie Glassman put it, "The basic poison is igno-rance, which means being totally in the dark, not seeing life as it is because of egocentric ideas." But, he continues, "If we are rid of the self, the three poisons become transmuted into the three virtues of the bodhisattva. Ignorance becomes the state of total nondiscrimination, so we no longer discriminate between good and bad; instead we deal with what is in the appropriate way. Similarly, anger becomes determination and greed becomes the selfless, compassionate desire of the bodhisattva to help all be-ings realize the enlightened way."

Peacock in the Poison Grove

When the monsoon started and the Buddha and his com-munity of monks and nuns gathered for the annual rainy season retreat, they would often hear the plaintive call of the peacock. Ever since then, this bird with its electric blue throat and tail strewn with eyes has captured the Buddhist imagination.

Peacocks are credited with being able to eat poisonous plants, snakes, and insects, and not only survive but thrive. For this reason, these boldly beautiful birds represent a particular way that we can relate to our mental and spiritual poisons.

In the Vajrayana tradition it's said that there are three ways of dealing with proverbial poison. The first, which is arguably the least dangerous option, is to avoid it. If you have a poison tree in your yard, chop it down. If you feel rage welling up in you, refrain from venting it. And if everyone else is drinking scotch, order apple juice.

But poison – if used correctly – can be a medicine, so maybe you'd like to put your axe down and let that tree in your yard live. It's important to remember, though, that you must be skillful to employ this method or else you simply end up poisoned. If you want to use the leaves of the poison tree as medicine, you need to know the correct dosage to use and the right time to take it. And if you want to use your so-called vices and unwholesome mental states as the path to enlightenment, you really need to know how to transform them.

Finally, in the third way of dealing with poison, we take a page from the peacock's playbook. The peacock struts over to that tree in your yard and just gobbles down a whole venomous branch because, to the peacock, poison is nothing other than nourishment. It's what creates the brilliant plumage.

Tenzin Wangyal, a lineage holder in the Bön Dzogchen tradition, puts the peacock's method into spiritual terms: "Instead of avoiding or manipulating poison, you host the poison. You bring naked awareness directly to the pain or poison, and discover that the true ground of being has never been poisoned. In so doing, the pain liberates by itself."

The Bird That Stormed Heaven

Fabulous and fantastical, Garuda is the lord of birds in both Buddhist and Hindu traditions. According to legend, Garuda had a five-hundred-year incubation and then hatched fully formed. His golden body was so luminous that he was mistaken for the god of fire and his wings beat with such vigor that the earth shook.

One day, Garuda's mother Vinata and her sister had a disagreement about the color of a horse's tail, and apparently this sister was quite testy, because to get revenge she kidnapped Vinata and held her ransom in a serpent-pit prison. *Amrita*, the nectar of immortality, was to serve as payment, and Garuda – desperate to free his mother – stormed heaven to steal it.

After that, however, things did not go quite as planned. Through subterfuge, Garuda completed his rescue mission, but the gods were hot on his heels and they eventually – with enormous effort – pried the amrita from his beak. In the fray, a few drops fell on some sharp blades of grass, and serpents licked these drops up, forever forking their tongues. Moreover, the god Vishnu managed to subdue Garuda and, taking him as his vehicle, granted him immortality.

Originally, Garuda was always depicted straightforwardly as a large, powerful bird. Later images, however, show him as a "bird-man." In Tibetan iconography, he has the torso and arms of a human, yet his thighs are feathered and culminate in talons and he has the fierce head of an eagle. It's said that his two horns symbolize the two truths, relative and ultimate, while his two angelic wings symbolize the union of method and wisdom. Because Garuda hatches fully mature, he represents the Vajrayana view that enlightenment can happen fully on the spot, without a long gestation. Because he extends his wings without limits and soars fearlessly into space, he represents absolute confidence.

As the lord of the skies, Garuda is traditionally seen as an enemy of the lion, the lord of the earth. But in the Tibetan imagination, the rivals mate and give birth to a beast that has the body of a lion and the wings and horns of Garuda. A symbol of the union of earth and sky, the Garuda-lion is one of what are called the three victorious creatures in the fight against disharmony. The other two are also born of animal enemies. The fish-otter's body is covered in the sleek, dark fur of an otter, but at the neck this fur gives way to scales. The *makara*-conch, on the other hand, is a dragonish water-monster, with its head and mane bursting from a spired shell.

Ikkyu's Crow

There is only one thing more magical than wildly impossible avian-mammalian hybrids – an absolutely ordinary bird. In 1420, Ikkyu, the celebrated Zen master, poet, and troublemaker, was meditating in a boat on Lake Biwa when he heard a crow cawing and found himself rattled into *satori*, an experience of enlightenment. "One pause between each crow's / reckless shriek Ikkyu Ikkyu Ikkyu," he wrote. "No nothing / only those wintery crows bright black in the sun."

Beyond being a pretty symbol, beyond being a character in a morality tale, birds are just what they are and they can reveal to us what we are. "All I am is the birds singing and fluttering," said the late meditation teacher Toni Packer. "Birdcalls and the songs of the breeze do not exist when the mind is full of itself."

Do you remember that dark, glossy creature that, for me, made a nest in the four noble truths? Well, almost as soon as class let out I found a friend who could tell me about my mystery bird, and, at first, I was disappointed by what I learned.

It was a European starling.

That is, of course, a lovely name. It has all the ancient allure of the Old World, plus – with a star – it's almost celestial. But European starlings are worse than ho-hum common birds; they're an invasive species stealing the nest holes of purple martins and swallows and nuthatches. They were introduced in 1890 when some harebrained humans decided to release sixty of them in Central Park because they wanted all the birds mentioned in Shakespeare's collected works to fly free in North America. Now, from Alaska to Central America, European starlings are perched on garbage cans pecking at moldy sandwiches; they're mobbing lawns; they're shitting dirty white on shiny cars. But this, all the same, is the truth: Sometimes – even if it's just for a moment – they still wake me up with their unmusical song.

Matthieu Ricard's Journey to Compassion

A Profile of Matthieu Ricard

In a tent made of woven yak hair, a thirteen-year-old girl was stirring cheese in a cauldron over a clay hearth as blue smoke from the fire escaped through an opening in the roof. Her father had died the year before, and now her mother had tuberculosis of the bone. She was so sick and frail that her eyes – too big for her gaunt face – had an oddly fixed look. Unable to afford the necessary lifesaving medicine, the girl's elderly grandmother was praying in a corner.

Matthieu Ricard, a French-born Buddhist monk and the founder of the non-profit organization Karuna-Shechen, came across this heartbreaking scene when he was visiting the nomadic communities of Eastern Tibet. Fortunately, he and his Karuna-Shechen team were able to help.

They gave the family a year's supply of medicine, and – as they explained how to administer it – the young girl listened carefully with both disbelief and hope flickering in her eyes. When the team returned a year later, they found the girl beaming. Her mother was still using makeshift crutches, but she'd recovered and was no longer skeletal and bedridden.

Karuna-Shechen, founded in 2000, has been the recipient of every penny of the royalties from Ricard's books, as well as any money he's earned from giving conferences or selling his fine-art photography. Ricard himself lives on a shoestring – he's slept in the same sleeping bag for thirty years and his retreat hut in Nepal has no central heating – but it's estimated that he's given one and half million dollars to Karuna-Shechen.

Other philanthropists have also contributed, and to date the organization has initiated and managed more than 140 humanitarian projects in Tibet, Nepal, and India. These include emergency relief to victims of earthquakes in Nepal, training illiterate village women in solar engineering, installing rainwater-harvesting systems in drought-prone regions, establishing a kitchen-garden program to combat malnutrition, and building new schools and improving existing ones.

"In this current era we are confronted with many challenges," Ricard writes in his new book, *Altruism: The Power of Compassion to Change Yourself and the World.* "One of our main problems consists of reconciling the demands of the economy, the search for happiness, and respect for the environment. These imperatives correspond to three time scales – short, middle, and long term – on which three types of interests are superimposed: ours, the interests of those close to us, and those of all sentient beings."

"Having more consideration for others is the most pragmatic way to deal with the challenges of our times," Ricard says. Indeed, "by meeting economists, environmentalists, psychologists, social workers, global shapers, and leaders, I realized that it is the *only* pragmatic answer."

From Thomas Hobbs to Ayn Rand, the idea that humans are essentially selfish and even brutish has dominated Western thought for centuries. Ricard, however, believes that human beings are innately compassionate and that we have the capacity to be more so. There are, he says, proven methods for systematically increasing compassion in ourselves and in our society.

While Ricard is fully aware that many people will dismiss his ideas as overly idealistic, he asserts that he's not just a nice-guy Buddhist monk who is fuzzy on facts. With sixteen hundred scientific references in *Altruism,* Ricard has science on his side.

Before Matthieu Ricard was a Buddhist monk, he earned a doctorate in molecular biology from the Institute Pasteur in Paris, where his main advisor was a Nobel laureate.

In 1966, when Ricard was twenty years old, his interest in Buddhism was triggered by some films about great Tibetan lamas who'd fled the Chinese invasion. Between his father, the philosopher Jean-François Revel, his mother, the painter Yahne Le Toumelin, and his uncle, the sailor/explorer Jacques-Yves Le Toumelin, Ricard had spent his whole life meeting accomplished, prominent people in a wide range of fields. Yet that didn't prepare Ricard for these lamas.

"Great artists, scientists, philosophers, and so forth are admired for particular skills, like painting, playing the piano, or solving mathematical equations," he says. The Tibetan Buddhist teachers, on the other hand, were skilled at being good human beings. In his words, he was "extremely inspired, extremely impressed."

Ricard got a cheap flight to India, where he met Tibetan Buddhist master Kangyur Rinpoche and spent three weeks living with him and his family in a two-room wooden hut in Darjeeling. At that time, Ricard did not speak Tibetan and barely spoke English, so he hardly understood a word of the teachings he heard. Nonetheless, he got a sense that Kangyur Rinpoche was a bit like the sun. "The sun allows all the crops to grow, all the fruits to mature," says Ricard. "It gives warmth but does not expect anything in return."

For six years, Ricard divided his time between the Himalayas and France, but he felt that this was like trying to sew with a two-headed needle or stay seated between two chairs. So, in 1972, after completing his dissertation on cellular genetics, he left behind his promising scientific career to dedicate himself fully to Buddhist study in Asia.

In his book *Happiness: A Guide to Developing Life's Most Important Skill*, Ricard describes Buddhism as never calling for blind faith. "It was a rich, pragmatic science of mind, an altruistic art of living, a meaningful philosophy, and a spiritual practice that led to genuine inner transformation," he writes. "I have never found myself in contradiction with the scientific spirit as I understand it – that is, as the empirical search for truth."

For twenty-five years, Ricard lived cut off from the wider

world – no radio, no newspapers. He studied intensively with Kangyur Rinpoche until his death in 1975, and then studied with the Dzogchen master Dilgo Khyentse Rinpoche, one of the twentieth century's most important Tibetan Buddhist teachers. He spent years in contemplative retreat.

Matthieu Ricard's quiet, anonymous life came to an end in 1997, when a publisher proposed that he and his father engage in a dialogue unpacking the meaning of life. Published as *The Monk and the Philosopher*, the book was a runaway success. More than 350,000 copies were printed in France and it was translated into twenty-one languages. Ricard was thrust into renewing his ties with the scientific world.

He engaged in a dialogue with astrophysicist Trinh Xuan Thuan, which was published as *The Quantum and the Lotus: A Journey to the Frontiers Where Science and Buddhism Meet*. He participated in meetings at the Mind & Life Institute, an organization inspired by the Dalai Lama that was founded to encourage dialogue between Buddhist scholars and scientists.

In 2000, Ricard's interests in science and compassion came together when he teamed up with neuroscientist Richard Davidson of the Center for Investigating Healthy Minds in Madison, Wisconsin. Ricard, in his words, "was a guinea pig" for cutting-edge research projects analyzing both the short- and long-term effects of training the mind through meditation.

For the first tests, he was confined in the noisy, claustrophobic clutches of an fMRI for more than three hours while he practiced several kinds of meditation: concentration, visualization, and compassion. For a lot of people, so much time in a machine of this type would be an ordeal that could easily lead to panic, but at the end of Ricard's grueling session, he emerged smiling. "That was like a mini-retreat!" he exclaimed.

The fMRI scans revealed that Ricard and other expert meditators – those who'd practiced for at least 10,000 hours – showed extraordinary levels of activity in the left pre-frontal cortex of the brain, which is associated with positive emotions. Activity in the right-hand side, which handles negative thoughts, was suppressed. When the results of the Madison experiments were released to the public, the media gave Ricard a memorable moniker. He became known as "the happiest man in the world."

"People often confuse happiness with pleasure," Ricard says. "Yet happiness is not eating ice cream. It's a way of being, and a way of being is not just one thing. It's a cluster of basic human qualities, among which inner freedom is central. If you're happy, you are not the slave of your rumination. You have freedom from hatred, obsessive craving, jealousy, arrogance, etc.

"That freedom gives you inner peace and, therefore, a confidence that's very different from narcissistic self-esteem. Because you have the inner resources to deal with life's ups and downs, you are less preoccupied with yourself. You know that whatever happens you'll be fine. So not feeling vulnerable, you are not trying to overprotect yourself, and you are naturally open to others.

"Selfish happiness doesn't exist," Ricard continues. "When you're completely self-centered – me, me, me all day long – you push away anything that could threaten your ego, threaten your comfort. This makes life miserable. You're constantly under threat, because the world is simply not a mail-order catalogue for all your desires."

Altruism, according to Ricard, does not require that we sacrifice our own happiness. In fact, a benevolent frame of mind, which is based on a correct understanding of interdependent reality, leads to a win-win situation. We flourish, and at the same time we are of benefit to all those around us.

Matthieu Ricard has been the Dalai Lama's French interpreter since 1989, and he recalls how, a few years ago, he was preparing to go on retreat in the mountains of Nepal when His Holiness gave him this advice: "In the beginning, meditate on compassion. In the middle, meditate on compassion. In the end, meditate on compassion."

To meditate on altruistic love and compassion, Ricard offers these simple instructions. "First you think about someone close to you," he explains. "You give rise to unconditional love and kindness toward them. Then you gradually extend this love to all beings, and you continue in that way until your whole mind is filled with love. If you notice this love diminishing, you revive it. If you become distracted, you bring your attention back to love."

"For compassion," he continues, "you begin by thinking of someone close to you who is suffering, and you sincerely wish for that person to be free of suffering. Then you proceed as you did for love."

Concern for others is a natural part of being human, says Ricard, yet it's also a skill we can cultivate. In *Altruism*, Ricard brings our attention to a pro-social game created at the University of Zurich, which gives people the opportunity to help another participant surmount an obstacle but at the risk of earning a lower score for themselves.

Two to five days prior to playing the game, participants either received a brief training in how to meditate on compassion or on how to improve memory. The experiment showed that participants who'd been trained in meditation were more likely to help. Moreover, an increase of pro-social behavior toward strangers was proportional to the period of time spent training in compassion.

Ricard says, "In the same way that a doctor trains for six to seven years to master his or her expertise, if you want to help others, it's not like you can just wake up in the morning thinking, 'I'm going to change the world.' You have to build up some qualities."

He stresses, however, that we need to understand this about compassion: If we lack compassion for some, we risk lacking compassion for all.

"If you have compassion for everyone but, say, a certain ethnic group or animals," he says, "then you are killing part of your empathic resonance with others. You end up dehumanizing a group of human beings or removing animals, say, from the sphere of your consideration."

"In order to progress toward a more altruistic society," Ricard writes in *Altruism*, "it is essential that altruists associate with each other and join forces. In our time, this synergy between co-operators and altruists no longer requires them to be gathered together in the same geographical location, since contemporary means of communication, social networks in particular, allow the emergence of movements of cooperation joining together large numbers of people who are geographically scattered."

In many aid organizations, people start with the good intention to relieve suffering, then they fall prey to human shortcomings, clashes of egos, and – worse – corruption. The humanitarian aid is derailed, ending up in someone's pocket or simply lost in bureaucratic chaos.

"The UN considers it a success if 50 percent of an NGO's funds reaches the people it should," says Ricard. But in the case of Karuna-Shechen, 98 percent of their funds reach their goal; only the remaining 2 percent is used to cover overhead. "I attribute this," Ricard continues, "to the fact that we at Karuna-Shechen all share the same vision, the same kind of training and dedication."

Karuna-Shechen recently offered three different vocational training workshops to women in India. The women were taught how to make candles and incense sticks, as well as two types of snacks. The most promising students were given further training and then, to get them off on the right foot, they were set up with a temporary candle-production unit.

The women now work from 10 a.m. until 4 p.m. six days a week and produce 150 candles a day in different colors and shapes – green Christmas trees, pink hearts, traditional Indian figurines. They receive the profits from selling their wares at local markets, plus they're paid an apprentice salary and their food and transportation costs are covered.

Rinku is one of the women now making candles. "Learning this new craft will not only help me start my own business, it will also improve my family's living conditions by adding income to our household," she says. "I will use part of the money to help pay for my siblings' education."

The women are proud to have been selected out of all of those who participated in the initial training session, because knowing how to make and sell wares can be the difference between having and not having a decent life. Employment opportunities for rural women are few, and what is available is usually backbreaking work, such as carrying bricks or spending long hours in fields under the pounding Indian sun.

With more concern for others, Ricard writes in *Altruism*, "We will all act with the view of remedying injustice, discrimination, and poverty." Furthermore, he says, "if we care about the fate of future generations, we will not blindly sacrifice their well-being to our ephemeral interests, leaving only a polluted, impoverished planet to those who come after us. We would on the contrary try to promote a caring economy that would enhance reciprocal trust, and would respect the interests of others."

While Matthieu Ricard is a champion of altruism and compassion, he is also blunt. He wants us to cultivate benevolence. Then he wants us to do more. "If compassion without wisdom is blind," he says, "compassion without action is hypocritical."

Be Love Now

A Q&A with Ram Dass

When *Lion Roar*'s editor-in-chief Melvin McLeod mentioned to me that he had been picked up hitchhiking by Ram Dass in 1973, I began to feel I was unqualified to do this interview. I wasn't alive in '73 when Ram Dass was driving around Vermont in a hippy van with images of Indian gods and gurus on the dashboard, and I certainly wasn't alive in '71 when his landmark book, *Be Here Now*, was published. But qualified or not, I wanted to do this interview. Ram Dass, born Richard Alpert, helped to shape a whole generation. He was a respected psychologist who, with his Harvard colleague Timothy Leary, became a psychedelic pioneer. Then, after Harvard saw fit to fire him for his drug experiments, he went India where he met and became a devotee of Hindu guru Neem Karoli Baba. Now, more than forty years later, Ram Dass is still on the same spiritual path and, he tells me, still growing spiritually. These days, due to the stroke he suffered in 1997, he speaks slowly and sometimes can't find a word he's looking for, but he remains articulate and his smile remains radiant. Our conversation was in honor of Ram Dass's book, *Be Love Now*.

How are you feeling?

I'm feeling wonderful.

Good to hear. But you've had some serious health problems. Have they aided or impeded your spiritual growth?

I think aging minimizes my desires, so that makes it easier to work on spirit. In total, I'd say that my health problems have helped me. Now that I'm aging I'm very content, and content-ment means good food for spiritual growth.

Why has service been an important part of your path?

Because of my guru. We worship Hanuman. Hanuman is a monkey, and he worships the deity Ram. Hanuman loves Ram only, and all he wants to do is serve Ram. My name is Ram Dass, meaning "Ram's servant." So service is my path. You serve with love everybody you can find. You feed them, nurture them, and do service. Service is a part of bhakti yoga.

How would you define bhakti yoga?

It's the yoga of the heart. It is a path of love – love of God, Ram, or your god. You're loving your god, you're loving your guru, you're loving.

It sounds so simple to love yet it's not. Why is it so difficult to be truly loving?

Because we are mind people and you can't love through the mind. The ego can't love – it's too anxious. We try very hard to love with our minds, but we can't do it. That's what our problem is.

Do you have any tips for making it easier to tap into love?

You can have my guru. He's up for grabs, and he'll love you until you bust.

In your book Be Love Now *you talk about faith and grace. How do you define these words?*

Faith is not belief. Belief is up here [taps temple], and faith is down here [taps heart]. Faith means you let other planes of consciousness in, for example, serendipity or things in your life that are not rational. You say, come on, come on. Grace is lubricating the well, the way. It's the way in which my guru, or God, makes my life graceful. It's light-hearted. My life was full of grace, and then I had the stroke, and all the people around me were like, "Tch, tch, tch, terrible, terrible, terrible." And I started to feel maybe it was terrible. But I talked to my guru inside, and I saw that it was grace. The stroke wasn't grace – the stroke was from nature – but the way I take it is grace.

You did a lot to shape the '60s and '70s. Where do you think the boomer/ hippie legacy stands now?

We added things to the culture. We added a lightness, and a playfulness, an inside-ness and spiritual-ness. I'm very happy we did all that. But then we made mistakes. The things we added were pushed in people's faces, and the culture responded from the right. There was a pendulum swing. If we had been a little quieter about what we were doing, maybe it would have been different, but we didn't want to be quiet. We didn't want to be quiet about psychedelics, and we didn't want to be quiet about the East and the powerful Eastern influence on our Western ways. Our legacy is not big, but it stands in the hearts of the people. It stands in our music.

It's great music!

Also, it stands in the movements that are creeping in – the environmental movement, the women's movement, the sexual freedom movement. And it stands in how many of us have gone to the East and have brought the East here.

Some people of my generation – Generation X – criticize Westerners who practice Eastern religions. They think it's silly to look to Eastern philosophy, or to Eastern teachers, as being a fount of wisdom that is superior to what we have here in the West. What do you think about that?

Eastern philosophy teaches us to go inward. In the West there's a god with a beard. In the East there's the god within, and the East meditates. Eastern cultures have always welcomed holy people, and we haven't in the West. You can go to a village in India, and they'll find you the holiest person they know. In our culture, it's all about the wealthiest person you know, the best-looking person. It's a different culture.

Recently here in the West, yoga, or rather the asana practice of hatha yoga, has become extremely popular. What are your thoughts about that?

I think that they miss the point of what yoga is about. They make it into body beautiful, and they make it worldly. Really, an asana is a conversation with god.

What are your thoughts about today's young people?

They are texting and multi-tasking. Now and then I meet a high school or a college student. Their hearts are okay.

Do you have a message for the younger generations?

Trust your intuition.

Thank you. Thank you very much for having this talk with me.

Instructions for the Home Cook

Dogen & My Galley Kitchen

According to Dogen, the thirteenth-century Buddhist master who founded the Soto Zen school in Japan, the position of *tenzo*, or monastery cook, is only suitable for someone who's highly realized. My condo is no monastery, so hopefully that means only a little bit of realization is required for me to do the family cooking. A little is all I have.

With two children under four and a full-time job, another thing I have little of is time and energy. As a result, my dinner solution is frequently to order pizza or Chinese food. Dogen would not approve. He was very clear: "Do not just leave washing the rice or preparing the vegetables to others but use your own hands, your own eyes, your own sincerity."

As all the Zen teachers agree, Dogen's classic text *Instructions for the Cook* is about more than making meals: it's a set of instructions for how to live. But I think I need to start small. I decide to see what happens if I bring just a taste of Dogen's teachings into my modern condo kitchen.

The cleaning side of kitchen work is not a major focus in *Instructions for the Cook*, but unless it is a major focus for me, I won't have any space for cooking. The compost has to be dumped. The tabletop is strewn with cracker crumbs and the dried, dark liquid of turtle beans. And the counters are piled with dirty dishes – pots, pans, a jumble of cutlery, a rainbow of sippy cups. Where do I even begin?

According to Dogen, "Put whatever goes to a high place in a high place and whatever goes to a low place in a low place so that, high and low, everything settles in the place appropriate for it."

This makes cleaning sound easy. "To place" is not the verb

of dirty work. Try "to scrub," or "to scour" – that's my reality. Frankly, I am suffering from deep kitchen ennui, and it's been going on for months. Even the thought of making a simple salad makes me feel exhausted, let alone mopping the kitchen floor.

I can almost hear Dogen say, "Get over it already." What he actually says is, "Day and night, the work for preparing the meals must be done without wasting a moment. If you do this and everything that you do wholeheartedly, this nourishes the seeds of awakening and brings ease and joy."

I take a breath, and another. Then I unpack and repack the dishwasher. It's a rare moment when my two kids aren't home, so working without one of them on my hip is a treat. Normally, during quiet times like this, I do my chores while talking on the phone or listening to stand-up comedy on Netflix. But under Dogen's tutelage, I now clean the kitchen whole-heartedly, without doing anything else.

Okay, truth be told, there is something else I'm doing simultaneously. I'm ruminating on my situation; I'm making a list of reasons why a monastery cook has it easy compared to me. Sure, a tenzo has to cook for more people, but monastics only eat twice a day, not three times (or more) like my ravenous family. Moreover, tenzos don't have small children clinging to them, so they have both their hands free for activities such as straining pasta. And tenzos don't have to listen to crying or referee fights over toys, so they can concentrate on things such as their cookbook instructions.

The cleaning goes on for so long that my useless thoughts of "It's so hard to be a parent," and "It would be so much easier to live in a monastery," simply burn themselves out. Meanwhile, it becomes clear that my condo is all about interbeing: the kitchen is not separate from the rest of the space; it's connected to the hall and the dining nook. Things that belong in the bedrooms or the TV room have ended up in the kitchen, and things that belong in the kitchen have ended up in the bedrooms or the TV room. In the end, I clean up bits and pieces of every room.

Finally, I find a knife and cutting board to make an Asian-inspired coleslaw. As I get out the ingredients, I think about Dogen's admonishment to care for them as I would care for the pupils of my own eyes. Since I would never slice or dice my own eyes, I don't quite know where to start. But Dogen says not to waste time. I need to get at it.

First up is the cabbage, which feels remarkably like a human head, not a pupil. I cut it in half and marvel at the almost perfect circle of a mandala that the cabbage forms. I could meditate on the soft yellow-green hues. A slightly darker shade rings the cabbage edge and then, just a few layers in, it quickly gives way to pale and paler rings.

Next up is the red pepper, with its shiny vermillion skin, light orange membranes, and tight clusters of seeds. The recipe calls for half a cup of sliced pepper. But treating it like my own eye is not just about appreciating its colors and textures. It's also – maybe more so – about not wasting it. I have a little more than I need, so I mound the measuring cup. I use every red scrap.

When my two toddlers come home, I'm still cooking. They are, as usual, hurricanes of activity, but the quiet time I've spent cooking and cleaning has relaxed me and I feel the full fierceness of my love for these pure little beings.

Dogen says, "Care for water and rice as though they were your own children." I say, one way to care for your children is by showing them your care for water and rice. And of course not just water and rice, but also carrots and onions, sugar and salt, and all the other ingredients in your kitchen.

I hand a whole lemon to my one-year-old son and let him explore the bright beauty of it. I pick up my two-year-old daughter and let her press the buttons on the food processor to grate the carrots, and then I let her taste everything.

Finally, when it's time to eat, one last Dogen passage plays through my mind: "When preparing the vegetables or ingredients, do not disparage the quantity or quality but instead handle everything with great care. Do not despair or complain."

I've always been lucky to cook with excellent and plentiful ingredients. So, in terms of food quantity or quality, I've had nothing to complain about, even if I were so inclined. But, I realize, I have disparaged the ingredients of my life, like my lack of time, my excess of stress.

Given the busyness of having two toddlers and a full-time job, I might need to order pizza tomorrow, but I realize that's okay. The greatest lesson that Dogen has dished up for me is appreciation.

Love – It's What Really Makes Us Happy

A Profile of Robert Waldinger

W hat makes life worth living? What really makes us happy? As a Zen priest and leader of the one of the most important studies of human happiness ever undertaken, Robert Waldinger has sought the answers to these questions.

What he's discovered is that science and Buddhism arrive at the same basic answer. They both conclude, he says, that "moving beyond the small self is a huge source of both meaning and contentment."

Waldinger is a clinical professor of psychiatry at Harvard University and director of the famed Harvard Study of Adult Development. It's perhaps the longest-running study of adult life ever conducted. For seventy-five continuous years, it has tracked the lives of 724 men in order to understand what makes for a healthy, happy life. Now it's following the next generation, as it tracks the lives of the original subjects' children and their families.

The study is one of the most important longitudinal research projects ever undertaken. Over the decades, the scientific community has followed the Study of Adult Development with interest, but the public was largely unaware of it and its findings about what really makes people happy and healthy. Then Robert Waldinger became an Internet star.

It started with a TED talk called "The Good Life." Waldinger expected to get only a few thousand views and was taken aback when the talk went viral.

Coca-Cola was the first company to get in touch: *Could Waldinger speak to executives in Romania in February?* After that, interview and speaking requests quickly flooded his inbox. Clearly, this was not when most people would power down. But that's what Waldinger did. With millions of viewers worldwide watching his talk, he took off for a three-week *sesshin,* a Zen retreat conducted largely in silence.

Between studying Buddhism and the lives of the 724 men, Waldinger has learned a thing or two about what's important in life – what creates happiness and what doesn't. And rather than just *knowing* the secret to the good life, he is trying to take the knowledge to heart and really *live* it. That's why Waldinger – at that intense moment in his career – stepped back to see what his intentions were.

"I have as much ego as anybody," he says. "When people are inviting you to do things and saying, 'Oh! We really want to hear from you,' it's a strange and heady experience. How do you not believe your own press release? How do you do something that has meaning?"

For Robert Waldinger, all the buzz meant one thing: It was time for quiet and reflection. Time for what really makes life worth living.

The Harvard Study of Adult Development began in 1938 as separate studies of very different populations. The first was focused on understanding healthy young adult development, so the researchers selected people they felt were the best and the brightest: a group of 268 sophomores at – surprise – Harvard. This cohort finished their studies during World War II and most went on to serve in the war.

The second study was started at Harvard Law School by a law professor and his wife, who was a social worker. They wanted to understand why some disadvantaged children went on to become delinquents, while others did not. They selected a group of 456 twelve- to sixteen-year-old boys from Boston's poorest and most troubled families.

When the studies were combined, all of the subjects were interviewed and given medical exams. The researchers went to the subjects' homes and interviewed their parents. And then life took its course.

The men went out into the world and became factory workers and lawyers, bricklayers and doctors. "Some developed alcoholism," Waldinger said in his TED talk, "a few developed schizophrenia. Some climbed the social ladder from the bottom all the way to the very top and some made that journey in the opposite direction." One of the Harvard cohort, John F. Kennedy, became president of the United States.

Over the years, some of the former tenement boys would ask, "Why do you keep wanting to talk to me? My life just isn't that interesting." But, Waldinger likes to quip, none of the Harvard grads ever asked that question.

Today, about sixty of the original 724 men are still alive and participating in the study. Most are in their nineties, and every two years the research staff calls them up and asks if they can send them one more set of questions about their lives.

Undoubtedly, the demographics of the study are problematic, since all of the original subjects were white men. About a decade ago, when the researchers first attempted to address the gender issue by inviting the men's wives to take part, many of the women chided them. "It's about time," they said. Now, in addition to the wives, the researchers are studying the men's more than two thousand grown children, and half of them are female. "Thank God!" says Waldinger.

Rectifying the lack of racial diversity is more complicated, since the focus of the second-generation study is understanding how the quality of a person's childhood affects his or her emotional and physical well-being in midlife.

"What we have that's so rare is information about the subjects' childhoods from their parents," says Waldinger. "I could collect a new, much more diverse sample of baby boomers and ask them what their childhoods were like and then measure their health now. That would be easy to do. But what we know about memory is that it's totally creative and faulty. When we remember our childhood, we leave out a lot and we make up a lot. Not because we're trying to, but because that's the way memory works."

Waldinger admits the study is imperfect and skewed, and that under other circumstances it would be shut down. But because of its detailed eyewitness reports, it is uniquely valuable.

After seventy-five years of studying people's lives, the clearest takeaway is this: over the long haul, strong relationships are what keep us healthy and happy.

In the early years of the study, this finding came as a surprise to the researchers. The idea that relationships are good for us is as old as the hills, but there wasn't proof that relationships are a good predictor for health, such as whether we get diabetes or heart disease in middle age. So, at first, the researchers thought they were just seeing some spurious correlation that didn't mean much. But it kept coming up, and then it started coming up in other peoples' research, too.

Eventually, the Harvard Study of Adult Development identified three key points about relationships and their benefit.

Loneliness Is Fatal

It's not just that social connections are good for us. It's that loneliness is fatal. People who are more socially connected are happier, healthier, and live longer than people who are less well-connected. Lonely people tend to experience a decline in their health earlier in midlife, their brain functioning degenerates sooner, and they live shorter lives.

Today, one in five Americans reports feeling lonely. This is an unprecedented epidemic of social isolation, one that has been decades in the making. When television worked its way into practically every home, social capital began to decline. Fewer people connected to their communities, joined clubs, went to church, or volunteered. "They simply stayed home and had passive experiences," says Waldinger.

Fast-forward to today and our lives are chockablock with screens. This, notes Waldinger, has further decreased social capital. "We don't talk to each other," he says, "we don't go out. So many people are feeling disconnected. Online connections can lead to real world connections, but they can also lead to a lack of real connection. You can have a thousand Facebook friends but still feel like there's nobody you can call if you are sick in the middle of the night."

If you're going through lonely times, Waldinger suggests you go and serve others who are also lonely. "What if you visited nursing homes? What if you made home visits to people who are shut-ins? What if you tutored people who can't read? There are so many ways that you could start connecting with people who need connection."

It's the Quality of Your Relationships That Counts

The second key point the study identified is that the quality of relationships is important.

While warm relationships are protective, high conflict marriages without much affection are toxic for our health, perhaps worse than getting divorced. In fact, how satisfied someone is in their relationships at age fifty is a better predictor of what their health will be at eighty than their cholesterol levels.

As Waldinger explains, "Good close relationships seem to buffer us from some of the slings and arrows of getting old. Our most happily partnered men and women reported, in their eighties, that on the days when they had more physical pain their mood stayed just as happy." On the other hand, people in unhappy relationships found that their physical pain was magnified by their emotional pain.

Good Relationships Are Good for Your Brain

The third key point is that strong relationships don't just protect our bodies; they protect our brains. People in their eighties experience earlier memory decline when they do not feel they have someone in their life they can count on in times of need. For octogenarians who do have such a person, their memories stay sharper longer.

In the field of psychology, feeling that you have one or more people you can depend on when the going gets tough is called being "securely attached." Keep in mind that being securely attached does not mean that your relationship is always smooth sailing. Some of the octogenarian couples Waldinger has studied could bicker with each other endlessly. But that hasn't taken a toll on their memories, as long as they feel securely attached to each other.

Often, we find secure attachment in a spouse or family member, but neither a marriage license nor blood ties is necessary. According to Waldinger, you just need to have the sense that there is at least one person in life you can really depend on to experience the health and well-being benefits of a relationship.

Studying people's whole lives – from childhood to old age – has given Waldinger a sense of how finite life is. He says that when you see the totality of a life from beginning to end, when you see there is nothing more for that person to become, it gives you a different perspective on life.

"What is really important? What do I want to be sure I do with this time, and what don't I want to do? Of course, we can all ask ourselves that question at any moment, but studying lives in this way makes me ask the question more often."

At the retreat he attended as his TED talk was going viral, Waldinger received transmission to teach Zen. After the ceremony, Waldinger felt he made a terrible mistake, and that he was the biggest imposter in the world. Yet it was also an absolute thrill. "It's a role I hope I grow into," he says.

"Zen is so much about *this* being our life – just this, whatever is coming up right now," says Waldinger. "It's brought more contentment to my life and has allowed me to step back from some of the things I'm so certain of, and then realize they aren't certain at all."

"Maybe there are religions that get to total happiness and bliss. But Zen doesn't work that way, and it certainly hasn't for me," he says. Happiness in the real world doesn't mean every day, every moment is happy.

Through meditation, Waldinger has gotten to know his own mind and body, and this knowing has been a source of frustration because, as he puts it, he watches his mind "do the same ridiculous things it's always done." But beyond the frustration, he's found more self-acceptance.

Waldinger laughs when he tells the story of having tea during that retreat. A little tray of snacks was being passed around and, from the end of the line, Waldinger was eyeing the one remaining brownie. "I found myself really wanting it and thinking, *Oh God! Who's going to take it?* Then I stopped and realized, *In a few hours, I'm going to receive dharma transmission, and all I can think about is whether I get that brownie!* Yep, this is what I do, and this is what I'm always going to do, but there's much less pain about it, much less agitation."

Being able to live a fortunate life depends a lot on luck – on having good health and having your loved ones with you. Circumstances can always change in a heartbeat. But right now, says Robert Waldinger, "I'm living a very fortunate life."

"One of the things that our participants talk about is the satisfaction from being involved in endeavors beyond the self," says Waldinger. "It might be nurturing their grandchildren. It might be making a beautiful garden. It might be volunteering in Africa."

Like the study, says Waldinger, Buddhist teachings also place a high value on relationships. In fact, *sangha*, community, is one of the "three jewels" of Buddhism, on par with the Buddha and the teachings.

Members of a spiritual community can support each other in practical ways, driving people to doctor's appointments or cooking them meals. And the relationship in community provides spiritual nourishment as well.

"Individually, we can get lost," Waldinger says. "We get caught up in worries and in being so sure that something needs to be different than it is. In community, we remind each other of truths that are easy to lose sight of – the truth of impermanence, the truth of no fixed self, the truth of everything being okay at a certain level just as it is."

Whether it's with our spiritual community, family, coworkers, or friends, there are ways we can improve our relationships. Maybe we can let go of our grudges and reach out to the family member we haven't spoken to in years. Maybe we can replace a little screen time with "people time," or liven up a stale relationship by doing something new together.

In Zen, it's said that in the expert's mind there are few possibilities, but in the beginner's mind there are many. What would happen if we were to bring fresh eyes to old relationships? What if we looked at our family members as if for the first time? "What if we brought beginner's mind to the family dinner?" asks Waldinger. "Often what happens is that relationships become ossified. We settle into roles and fixed images of the other, but of course those images are distortions."

According to Waldinger, one of the most powerful tools for improving our relationships is meditating. Through meditation, we get to know ourselves, and when we truly understand our own minds and bodies, we understand a lot about other people's minds and bodies too. That makes us more compassionate with ourselves and everyone around us.

Finding Light in the Darkness

A Q&A with Robert Jay Lifton

Genocide, totalitarianism, atrocity – psychiatrist and author Robert Jay Lifton studies the worst in human nature to help us bring out the best. Among his seminal works are *The Nazi Doctors: Medical Killing and the Psychology of Genocide; Death in Life: Survivors of Hiroshima; Thought Reform and the Psychology of Totalism: A Study of Brainwashing in China;* and *Superpower Syndrome: America's Apocalyptic Confrontation with the World.* His reflections on the darkest deeds of modern life – and the values that can help us prevent them – make him an essential moral and political voice in a world frightened about its future.

Has studying the worst manifestations of evil of modern times made you feel hopeless about the future?

No, I'm not a hopeless person. In confronting these issues, I'm expressing the possibility of alternatives. I feel we have the potential for evil behavior but also the potential for something better. I never expect quick results, but I feel that a scholar like myself has an obligation to be an activist. So I do these studies as an act of hope.

How do you cope emotionally with immersing yourself in atrocities?

My way of dealing with it is to not be overly single-minded about it. I say, with some whimsy, to my students and friends, "Don't read this stuff after nine o'clock," but I mean it with some seriousness. I need to pace myself like an athlete so that I have some sense of my limits. Another part is having a lot of love around and a life quite removed from the research. That doesn't mean that it doesn't remain with me and have its costs, but those are some of my ways of coping.

After studying Nazi doctors, you said that socializing people to do evil is relatively easy. But I feel I'd never do what those Nazi doctors, for example, did. Am I wrong?

You may be right. Socialization to killing is a grave danger, but that doesn't mean it's impossible to resist. It means that resistance takes an exceptional moral imagination, and here and there I've encountered that. In the case of the Nazis, much of the dirty work was done by people who weren't fanatical ideologues. They were people who were brought into and adapted to an environment in which some kind of wrong was the norm. The ability to resist often had to do with understanding in advance what the Nazis were about, and therefore anticipating what an adaptation to them would entail.

During World War II you believed that the United States stood for progressive policies and decency in the world. Do you feel that now?

I grew up believing in my country and in the integrity and compassion of its leaders. That is no longer the case. It's quite the reverse in terms of our leaders now. A democratic society can't be absolute protection against extreme ideologies that can appear within it, and that's what's happening in our society. Having said that, I still love my country and recognize the opportunities I've been given to have an unusual career that could only occur here. I also have great hope for our resilience and for calling upon what Lincoln called "our better angels" – in this case, our more humane institutions to right our moral compass and turn things around. That's what I try to work for.

In your book, Superpower Syndrome, *you explore how the beginning of the twenty-first century is characterized by "apocalypticism." Can you tell me about that?*

The apocalyptic impulse has to do with destroying much of the world in order to purify and recreate it in some sort of perfect form. Often, we think of our opponents, like bin Laden and others, as manifesting apocalypticism, but we've got our share of it at home. Some of the Christian radical right press for Armageddon – an end of the world so that the world can be recreated and Jesus can return. That sounds wild, but it's not absent from the centers of power. There is also a secular apocalypticism on the part of people in high places who aren't necessarily religious but who feel the need for American hegemony in the world and for the destruction of all that interferes with the reconstruction of the world in a perfect American form

You say this idea of purification and renewal is the foundation of all totalitarianism.

Yes, all totalitarian societies are societies that call upon an apocalyptic idea that involves destroying all that is impure. Of course, they define what constitutes impurity in their own ways – communists might define it one way, fascists another way, and religious fanatics still another. But they all have in common the idea of recreating the world in some form of self-defined perfection.

You once said that survivors of atrocities go one of two ways. They either shut down and become incapacitated or they confront their experiences and derive insight from them. What is the insight survivors can potentially gain?

Usually it has to do with suffering and evil. If survivors have the strength, they can draw upon their knowledge and find meaning in the destructive force. Then they can engage in a survivor mission toward helping the world avoid that kind of event again. A good example is Hiroshima survivors who have found a survivor mission by traveling around the world to warn people about what nuclear weapons can do. There have also been parallel examples of Vietnam veterans back in the 1970s who were able to reveal the truth about their war and take a stand against it.

But what makes one survivor go one way and another survivor go the other?

There is no single reason. Partly it has to do with the environment that one returns to — how much it can nurture some quest for humane meaning or how much it may do the opposite and be itself involved with violence. It also has to do with one's previous experiences — what one grew up knowing about war and peace and about threat and suffering. They might have had certain moral or religious principles to which they return. That's why collective forms of knowledge or collective principles of morality — both religious and secular — have such enormous importance. They attract people toward expressing what is most humane in them individually.

I understand that your sense of ethics began in a secular form and has remained secular, but that it also has a spiritual component. Can you tell me about that?

I've worked closely with various anti-war and anti-nuclear Catholics, including the Berrigan brothers, and I've worked similarly with anti-war and anti-nuclear Protestants and Jews, many of them religious leaders. I find in common with them a passion to oppose destructive behavior and prevent suffering. That passion has a spiritual component. That stays with me and it becomes inseparable from my activities and my writings, but it has never been part of a religious belief system. Some of my friends feel that as a Jew I'm expressing certain Jewish principles, but I am a secular Jew and so if I am expressing Jewish principles, they are something that is in me rather than part of an idea structure.

How has your research taught you to live your own life?

You'd probably have to ask my family! But I'd like to believe that the experiences I've had with my research have deepened my dialogue with people in general and with young people in particular. I recognize the vulnerability and extraordinary power of the young.

Deer to the Heart

Why the Deer Listened to the Buddha

S omehow, I'd missed the part about the deer.
I'd read everything in the guidebook about Nara, or at least I thought I had. I'd read that Nara's temple Todai-ji sheltered a gargantuan bronze statue of the Buddha, the largest of its kind in the world, and that, on the outskirts of the city, there was a pleasant hiking trail, which meandered past tea fields and a scattering of Buddhist sculptures.

One sweltering summer day, I was on holiday from my job teaching English in Osaka, so a friend and I took the train to Nara. Minutes after we arrived, we were on a busy street when we saw not one but several deer. And they did not have the classic deer-in-headlights look. They were not afraid.

I was astounded; I had never before seen deer in the bustling heart of a city. As I pointed and squealed, various Japanese people flashed me with bemused smiles. Clearly, they were not surprised that there were deer prancing on Nara's sidewalks.

Deer, I was to learn, have a long history in Nara. According to legend, Shinto god Takemikazuchi-no-mikoto rode into the city on the back of a white deer. In 768 C.E., the shrine Kasuga-taisha was established in Nara to honor Takemikazuchi-no-mikoto as well as several other Shinto gods, and ever since that time the gods have been sending messengers in the form of deer to protect the city. While it was a crime punishable by death to kill one of Nara's sacred deer until the seventeenth century, they lost their sacred status after World War II and were designated as National Treasures.

The fact that I missed any mention of deer while planning my trip to Nara seems to me now as indicative of how I thought about deer in general. That is, I virtually never thought about them. Not being shellfish or dogs or cockroaches, deer were not animals that I ate or loved or despised. I knew they were associated with the hunt – the gentle, noble, wild victims of it – and I didn't feel a connection to that image. If deer were anything at all to me, they were simply the fleeting view of their hindquarters disappearing into some thicket. And that was rare; I was, and still am, a city-dweller.

But in Nara, coming face to face with so many dappled, perky-tailed deer, I felt forced to consider them, both as spiritual symbols and as living, breathing creatures. In either case, I discovered, deer are not one thing, not easy to pin down. They are complex, dynamic.

Deer are native to every continent except Australia and Antarctica and live everywhere from prairies to mountains, from tundra to tropical rainforests. Molting twice a year, they wear thin summer coats and thick winter ones, and these coats range from foxy red to chocolate brown and sometimes even lean toward grey. The world's most diminutive deer is the northern pudu, which when fully grown can weigh as little as 7.3 pounds. On the other end of the cervid spectrum is the moose, standing at 8.5 feet and weighing up to a whopping 1,800 pounds.

Deer are ruminants, cud-chewers with four-chambered stomachs, but some will consume meat if it's available. With long, powerful legs, deer are excellent swimmers, jumpers, sprinters. They have large ears, always cocked to danger, and with the exception of Chinese water deer, all male deer sport antlers, be they simple spikes or ornate branches.

In art, deer first reared their antlered heads in Paleolithic cave paintings. Later, they lent their noble spirit to heraldry and leapt into literature. "A wounded deer leaps the highest," wrote Emily Dickinson. "Three times it cried out/but now not heard anymore,/a deer in the rain," wrote Buson. And, of course, there was Bambi.

In Old and Middle English, the word "deer" (that is, deor and der respectively) simply meant animal, suggesting that the deer was an animal of particularly meaty importance. In other words, while I enjoy going to the supermarket and purchasing avocadoes and tins of tuna, my ancestors did not have that luxury. By necessity, the deer as a symbol of the hunt was, for them, deeply evocative.

Deer hold a place in mythological and spiritual traditions from around the world. But being a Buddhist I'm particularly fascinated by their role in Buddhism.

First and foremost, in Buddhism, deer symbolize the Buddha's most essential teachings and the act of receiving them. After all, it was in the Deer Park that the Buddha taught for the very first time. When we see a doe and buck flanking a dharma wheel, we are reminded that the Buddha taught in order to save all beings, not just humans.

Deer are also well represented in the Jataka Tales, which are fantastical parables attributed to the Buddha and which deal with his previous incarnations – human and animal. We don't need to believe that these tales are historically accurate in order to understand their message of wisdom and compassion.

The Deer Listened

After awakening, the Buddha hesitated. Should he teach, or shouldn't he? Would anyone else ever be able to understand the truth that he'd discovered? Yes, he finally decided, some – very few – would listen. And some – even fewer – would awaken. He needed to teach for them.

The Buddha made his way to Deer Park in Sarnath, a place close to Varanasi that deer frequented, in order to find his five former companions. For six years, the Buddha had practiced austerities with them on the banks of a river. In hope of gaining enlightenment, he had meditated incessantly, starved himself until he was skin and bone, and limited his breathing until his head had felt like it would split open. Eventually, however, he'd realized that self-deprivation would never lead to awakening, only death. His abandoning asceticism had been a great disappointment to his five companions and so they tried to ignore him when he arrived at Deer Park.

But they couldn't. They couldn't ignore him because he was visibly changed. In his bearing, there was an uncanny peacefulness, an extraordinary dignity. The five ascetics sat before the Buddha and received his teachings. Deer were present and, it is said, they too listened.

The first noble truth that the Buddha taught is that there is suffering. Our suffering is like an illness and if we are ever to cure it, we first need to acknowledge it. Often, our suffering is subtle – more like vague dissatisfaction. Sometimes, it is extreme.

The second noble truth is that we suffer because of our craving and fundamental ignorance. We cling to our misguided belief that we are a separate, independent self and – struggling against the natural challenges in life – we strive to get something better for "me." This struggle is painful and futile. Our ego can never get enough.

The third noble truth is simply that a way out of suffering exists, and the fourth is that the way out is via the eightfold path: wise understanding, wise intention, wise speech, wise action, wise livelihood, wise effort, wise concentration, and wise mindfulness. In short, the Buddha taught that if we live ethically, meditate, and cultivate wisdom, we have the potential to discover freedom from suffering, just as he did.

It strikes me as richly symbolic that deer – so often hunted and sacrificed – were present when the Buddha proclaimed that he taught suffering and the end of suffering. Buddhism teaches that when we experience pain it is like being shot by an arrow. If we don't resist the pain, all we feel is that one arrow, but when we do resist it, it's as if we have shot ourselves with a second arrow. That second arrow is our suffering. Arrows, here, are a metaphor, yet for deer arrows can be very literal. Deer know suffering intimately and so perhaps it was that knowledge that drew them to listen when the Buddha taught. I like to picture their

large, velvety ears wholly cupped to him and the first turning of
the wheel.

Who Is the Deer?

Of all the Jataka Tales, this is one of the most widely known
and most poignant:

Nigrodha was a bright-eyed stag with silvery horns and
a golden hide. He led a herd of five hundred deer, while Sakha,
another handsome stag, was the leader of a similarly large herd.
To satisfy one king's hunger for meat, both herds were driven
into a stockade.

Every day, the king's hunters went to the stockade for the
purpose of shooting and killing one deer for the king's table.
Nigrodha and Sakha were such magnificent beasts that the king
granted them immunity from this fate, but all the other deer suffered terribly. Every day, as the arrows rained down, there was
terror and chaos. Many deer were injured and sometimes there
was more than just the one required death.

Nigrodha proposed a system to prevent unnecessary suffering. The deer that was to die would be selected by lottery. One
day, the deer would hail from Nigrodha's herd, then the next day
from Sakha's. The selected deer would go without struggle to his
or her death in order to keep the others safe. The deer followed
this system until one day a pregnant doe from Sakha's herd found
herself chosen to die.

The doe went to Sakha and begged him to spare her life until her fawn was born and old enough to fend for himself. Sakha,
however, was hard with her and said that there was no room for
mercy in this system.

In desperation, the doe went to Nigrodha and implored him
to intervene. "It is unfair that two should die instead of one," he
agreed. "You are safe until your fawn is born and thriving."

When the time came for the slaughter, Nigrodha offered
himself in the doe's place. The king – in awe that Nigrodha

would make this sacrifice for a deer who wasn't even in his herd –
immediately proclaimed that he would spare the life of Nigrodha
as well as the doe.

"No," said Nigrodha, "I won't be spared if that will put another deer in jeopardy of being selected for slaughter."

Again, the king was awed and humbled by Nigrodha's depth
of compassion and, with that, he promised to forever forgo hunting deer, whether inside the stockade or in the wild.

"No," said Nigrodha, "we won't be spared if that means that
you will hunt other animals all the more."

And with that the king promised to forever forgo hunting
any type of beast, and from that day forward the entire kingdom
was a place of refuge for every creature great and small.

Tradition tells us that when the Buddha concluded this
tale, he claimed that in a previous life he was Nigrodha, while
his brother-in-law Devadatta was Sakha and his cousin Ananda
was the king, and his student Kumara-Kassapa was the doe's
offspring.

Who are all of these people? For me, that's not the important question. What's important is who am I; who are you?

Here is what I think of as something of a Jataka Tale from
my own life:

My father was a hunter in a long line of hunters.

He and my mother were divorced, and I lived with her. I
only visited my father in the summers, outside of hunting season.
So, though I was familiar with his rifles and the bony boar jaw he
kept on his desk, I never saw fresh kill. Except once.

One summer when I arrived, there was a deer dangling from
the garage ceiling. Hanging by its legs, the doe's position felt jar-
ringly wrong; her stillness was eerie. I couldn't bring myself to
touch the soft hide; I could barely bring myself to look at her.

So that's the end of my Jataka Tale. Now, who is the deer in
this story? Who is the hunter? And who is the girl?

The answer, I have reluctantly come to admit, is that they are all me. I am the hurting deer, subject inevitably to that eerie stillness, and I am the human hunter, hurting others in my ego-fueled ignorance. And, also, I am the girl. The girl who doesn't "feel a connection to the hunt." The girl who would rather look away.

Now, who are you in the story?

And when will you and I be ready to listen – really listen – to the Buddha's teachings?

Feminine Principal

Trudy Goodman, Pat Enkyo O'Hara, and Palden Drolma – Three Women Buddhist Teachers

I n a hospital room in Buffalo, New York, Trudy Goodman had a spiritual experience she had no way to understand.

Goodman was only twenty-one at the time, and her then husband was not much older. So young, so inexperienced, they knew nothing about childbirth. While she was wracked by contractions, he felt helpless and started to read. But it was incongruous – his book, her pain. Goodman lost her patience and told her husband to leave. For the next four hours, she labored alone. Only a nurse checked in on her every hour or so .

In her aloneness, in her intense pain, Goodman discovered a "pinnacle of now-ness," she says. It was vast. It was deep. It was her realizing her connection to every being who had come before and to every being who would ever follow.

Two years later Goodman was in a hospital in Geneva, Switzerland. Her two-year-old daughter had suddenly fallen ill with spinal meningitis, and the doctors said that she was dying. One day, there were six doctors crowded around the tiny, sick body in the bed, and Goodman found herself experiencing another profound opening. After that she started searching for answers, delving into the teachings of mystics and yogis. "They'd say, 'Eat artichokes,'" she tells me, "they'd say this and that." But it never felt right. Then her childhood friend Jon Kabat-Zinn invited her to a talk by the Korean Zen master Seung Sahn.

"That first time I heard him speak, I saw that he knew what I knew and he knew what I needed to know," says Goodman. It was something in his eyes, rather than anything he said. "In fact," she continues, "Seung Sahn spoke pidgin-English. He said, 'The sky is blue, the grass is green.' Real simple Zen talk, but I remember crying. Just weeping with relief, feeling like I'd come home. That's how I met the dharma."

Today, more than three decades later, Trudy Goodman is the founder and guiding teacher of InsightLA, a community in Los Angeles that offers daily sitting groups, weekend retreats, and a variety of Buddhist and secular mindfulness classes. She's committed to making meditation practice available to people with busy, urban lives, but without turning the practice into what she calls "McMindfulness." As she describes it, her teaching style is "Vipassana with a strong Zen flavor."

When Goodman began studying the dharma in the 1970s, there were very few women Buddhist teachers. Among prominent teachers, a gender imbalance still exists today, yet it is cause for celebration that here in the West, women are increasingly taking their place at the podium.

Some Buddhists claim that to emphasize the importance of women teachers is to genderize the dharma. They believe that the dharma is the dharma and, therefore, it doesn't matter if it's a man or a woman teaching it. But if gender doesn't matter, then why shouldn't there be more women teachers? Why have women been excluded? As scholar Rita Gross said of the work of Buddhist feminists, "We're not genderizing the dharma. We're un-genderizing it. The dharma was genderized thousands of years ago when women were first put in a separate class."

The Buddha praised his female students for their wisdom and founded an order of nuns. Yet after his death, when a council of five hundred *arhats* (perfected saints) gathered to establish the Buddhist canon, not one *arhati* (female arhat) was among them. Over the millennia there have been women teachers, but seeking them out is like seeking scraps. While Buddhism's male ancestors fill lists, in each tradition there are only a handful of known female ancestors.

Buddhist culture, however, is not static. It changes with each culture it encounters. India, China, Tibet, Vietnam – the role of Buddhist women has shifted according to place and time, and it has shifted again while taking root in the West. When Buddhism came to America in the 1960s and '70s, it encountered the burgeoning movement of second-wave feminism. People – both women and men, both Western and Asian – began questioning power dynamics within sanghas. They began working to make chants and liturgy gender neutral, to call for female ordinations where they had previously been denied, and to encourage women to assume leadership roles. Today in the West one of the most celebrated Buddhist teachers is a woman – Pema Chödrön – and there are a host of others who are likewise making a significant contribution to the dharma. Among them are Trudy Goodman, Roshi Pat Enkyo O'Hara, and Lama Palden Drolma.

Trudy Goodman's heart teacher was Maurine Stuart, one of the first female Zen masters in the United States and also a mother of three, a concert pianist, and a piano teacher. "Maurine had a full, balanced life," says Goodman. "She modeled that it's possible to do intensive spiritual practice while living as a lay-woman and still do·your hair and joke about new lipstick. I loved her and did very deep practice with her."

It was important to Goodman to have a woman teacher because, although she'd been immediately drawn to Buddhism and what she believed was its profound vitality and clarity, she had nonetheless felt that the teachings she'd been receiving from men didn't relate enough to the things that ordinary women like her really cared about. Things, says Goodman, like "our work in the domestic sphere, our relationships, our family lives, how to balance work and family."

Goodman found the teachings that sprang up after the time of the Buddha to be the most problematic. For instance, meditation instructions for working with desire became misogynistic over the centuries. The Buddha taught us to imagine what we'd find if we peeled off our skin – to imagine the red mess of our blood, liver, kidneys. The idea was that if we mentally dissect our body, we will cut through our attachment to our own physical form and by extension to the physical form of others. Later teachers, however, sometimes gave instructions to imagine the body of a woman stripped of skin, so it was her disgusting guts revealed, not the male meditator's. The view of women as sinful and impure served the monastic community, says Goodman, because it helped monks maintain their celibacy.

"It's a rich area of practice to look at how our gender and sexual orientation affect our perceptions and how these perceptions affect our relationship to the teachings," Goodman tells me. Very often, she says, sexuality is outside of our awareness; we compartmentalize it. But we can look deeply at our thoughts and actions, and our mindful awareness can encompass our sexual behavior. Do we exempt our sexual fantasies when tracking the ways that attraction, aversion, ignorance, and delusion are affecting our practice? How do we integrate our practice into our relationships? And even when we're in a celibate phase of our lives, are we aware of how we react to manifestations of sexual behavior in art and the media and have we made peace with our own past behaviors?

"I'm very interested in the integration of sexuality and relationship in dharma practice," says Goodman. "A sense of being embodied is harder to escape for women. We have periods. We give birth. There's blood and milk. Our bodies are dynamic and powerful."

About two years prior to discovering the dharma, Goodman began undergoing psychoanalysis. Then she started sitting and was struck by the synergy between the work she was doing with her analyst and the work she was doing on the cushion. "They're both awareness practices," she says. "In meditation we focus more on awareness of how the mind works, while in therapy we also bring attention to the content of our experience. Sitting and therapy work beautifully together. Together you have a full-spectrum human being."

Goodman was inspired to become a psychoanalyst and worked in that field for twenty-five years, practicing mindfulness-based psychotherapy even before it was called that. She also led and attended Buddhist retreats and, in the process, noticed a pattern emerge. On the Monday after a retreat, she'd go back to her office and all her clients would have an opening or breakthrough in their therapy. She says: "At first I thought, wait a minute, how can this be? But it happened over and over. There was no question that when I became freer inside, it allowed everyone who consulted with me to step into that freedom and benefit. I wasn't practicing just for me."

Goodman has practiced Theravada, Zen, and Vajrayana and, according to her, early Buddhism, or the Theravada tradition, contains everything that you find in the later teachings of Zen and Vajrayana. "Early Buddhism has it all," she says. From the koans of Zen to the Dzogchen practices of Vajrayana, the same principles are expressed in different forms, with certain things emphasized more or less. She concludes: "I've experienced a lot of joy at seeing the creativity and cultural sensitivity of each tradition."

Roshi Pat Enkyo O'Hara is the abbot of the Village Zendo, located in the heart of Manhattan. "If you come to sit with us early in the morning, it's very quiet," says O'Hara. "Then it gets very noisy, and you are never not aware that you are in the middle of one of the biggest cities in the world. When you step out onto Broadway, there are droves of people walking up and down the street – some happy, some sad. You know you're a part of this vast, interconnected universe, and you're aware of your responsibility in the world. I think that's one of the reasons we at the Village Zendo are so socially engaged."

In 1986, O'Hara co-founded the zendo with her partner Barbara Joshin O'Hara. The couple had been practicing at Zen Mountain Monastery in the Catskills but they wanted a place to sit in the city as well. So, it wasn't "a center" per se that they set out to establish, just a community of people who would support each other in their practice. Nonetheless, the community grew exponentially and O'Hara's teachers encouraged her to make it a more formal center. O'Hara complied. Yet, in terms of organizational structure, the original flavor of the sangha has remained. The sangha began as a community effort and this is still true. That's not to say, however, that the Village Zendo is without leaders and decision makers; all organizations need these roles fulfilled in order to function, and the zendo is no exception. O'Hara is the head teacher, but five other teachers work close-ly with her on teaching strategy, and each teacher – including O'Hara – has just one vote. "I respect them and they respect me," she says. But "they can vote me down – and have." The zendo also has a democratically run executive committee and a board to deal with the administrative functioning. This relatively flat organiza-tional structure reflects O'Hara's political philosophy.

Before she practiced at Zen Mountain Monastery, O'Hara went to several Buddhist centers that made her uncomfortable. They were too hierarchical, too sober, too restricted. "In various communities you have the people in power and the people not in power," she explains. Of course, women are not the only ones adversely affected by these dynamics. But, as a woman, O'Hara is sensitive to power differentials and the damage they can cause. Women are frequently aware of having been pushed aside and, as such, are sensitized to the issue of power. "I think it changes the way communities function when there's female leadership," she says. "Male teachers are often the seat of all the knowledge, all the power, all the talk. You don't see that so much with women teachers."

In her career as a professor, O'Hara was likewise concerned with power differentials. For twenty years, she taught at New York University's Tisch's School of the Arts, where she co-founded a program called interactive media. At the time of its founding, before the age of the Internet, it was revolutionary. In the beginning the program focused on using split-screen televi-sions as a way for people to talk to each other.

"The communication wasn't one-way," she says, "and that

was the key to a more horizontal power structure, to elevating a population and putting it on an equal status with the people in power. One of the first projects we did was in a little town in Pennsylvania, where we connected all the senior citizen centers to the mayor's office. Then once a week the seniors would interview the mayor and it would go out on the cable system for the whole county."

Later O'Hara worked with other marginalized populations, including kids in a drug treatment center to whom she taught videography. For people with drug issues, particularly those dealing with addiction to crack and other hard narcotics, the ability to pay attention has been eroded. In order to interview one another or to hold a camera, O'Hara's young students first needed a certain level of attention, and so she taught them meditation. They started with a minute or two of trying to follow the breath and built up from there – the incentive of getting to use the camera keeping them going. "I loved that project," says O'Hara. "In the beginning the kids just talked. They didn't know how to do an interview." But in the end, they learned to listen to one another.

Another major element of O'Hara's work at NYU was to mentor new artists – to help students enrolled in the school to develop their voice in media. Today mentoring continues to be important to her. Her focus has shifted, however, to nurturing a new generation of Buddhists engaged in social issues. One example is that she is the spiritual director of the New York Zen Center for Contemplative Care (NYZCCC), a non-profit that offers a Buddhist Chaplaincy Program and provides direct care to the sick and dying.

Koshin Paley Ellison, a co-founder of NYZCCC, has a deep appreciation for O'Hara's patience with people, process, and unfolding. He says, "Over the past two decades, she's taught me a lot about trust – trusting that each person will find their practice, that each person will find where they need to go."

The essence of contemplative care is being with someone where they are and not trying to get them to change. "One of the huge struggles that many of our beginning chaplaincy students have is feeling like they need to 'do' something," Ellison continues. "They feel the need to fix somebody. They need to get busy. But Roshi O'Hara's teaching is not about that. It's about being with the moment in an unadorned way. It's learning how to trust that you are enough. You don't need to go into a patient's room and perform tricks. You just need to show up with your whole body and mind."

O'Hara teaches that the very heart of Zen practice is becoming intimate with yourself. "Once you really know yourself," she says, "then, automatically, you are available to serve the world."

In her early twenties, Lama Palden Drolma liked to go to a ramshackle garden in her Californian neighborhood. There, she'd stand facing a statue of the Virgin Mary and pray for help in finding her true teacher.

As long as Drolma could remember, she'd been on a spiritual path. She says that even at age three she had powerful dreams of her past lives – dreams that reminded her of her purpose for this lifetime. Growing up, Drolma was uncomfortable in America. She lived with her family in an affluent neighborhood in the Bay Area, and on the surface the lifestyle was picture perfect, yet the beautiful houses and high-powered jobs didn't create happiness. In her early teens, Drolma began to feel an intense spiritual longing. In high school, she studied comparative religion and in university she delved deeply into Zen, esoteric Christianity, and Sufism. Then, when Drolma was twenty-five, a Sufi friend took her to a talk by the Tibetan Buddhist master Kyabje Kalu Rinpoche, and Drolma immediately recognized him as her teacher. That night she took refuge with him and six months later she moved to his monastery in the Himalayas.

Conditions there were rough. "If you washed your clothes – which you had to do in freezing cold water – and then you hung them up in your room, after ten days they would still not be dry," she says. The fog was that thick. As for good food and hot baths, they were a bus-ride away in Darjeeling. Nonetheless, Drolma barely noticed the hardship. Being with her teacher made her feel completely at home.

Kalu Rinpoche often spoke about how religions manifest in different ways, depending on the culture that gives birth to them, but all in their essence are reflections of awakened mind. This teaching resonated with Drolma and she relates it to her belief in a universal awakened feminine. As she puts it, the Virgin Mary, Guanyin, Buffalo Woman, and Saraswati are all different faces of this same feminine energy.

In 1982, Drolma began a three-year closed retreat under Kalu Rinpoche on Salt Spring Island in British Columbia. "It was the best, most useful thing I have ever done in my life," she says. "It was also extremely challenging. I had to face the difficulty of my own mind, my own aspirations, my own negative habitual patterns. Then my younger brother died and it was excruciating-ly hard not to be able to be there with my family. But the hardest thing about my three-year retreat was that my son was ten years old at the time. He stayed with my mother and it was difficult to be apart from him."

This sacrifice of not being with her child made Drolma feel like she had to make the most of her retreat and she prac-ticed with vigor. As a result, a shift occurred in her; the spiritual longing she'd been feeling since her teens dissipated. "My heart reconnected with itself in the deepest way," she explains. "There wasn't anything to long for anymore. There was nothing sepa-rate from me spiritually."

A year after the completion of the retreat, Drolma was authorized as a lama, or teacher, making her one of the first Western female lamas in the Vajrayana Buddhist tradition. She moved to Marin County, California, and began teaching in her living room. But her students quickly outgrew the space and in 1996 she founded Sukhasiddhi Foundation, a center dedicated to the study and practice of Tibetan Buddhism.

"Kalu Rinpoche authorized some women as lamas who have

still never really taught," says Drolma. Vajrayana Buddhism is basically still "a boys' club," she continues, so it's intimidating for women to assume teaching roles. "Women being supported is really a key issue. I think if my parents hadn't been supportive of me and Kalu Rinpoche and all my other teachers hadn't been 100 percent supportive, I would never have become a teacher."

According to Drolma, there's a difference between rinpoches who have a lot of realization and what she calls the "middle management lamas," who aren't as realized and are more culturally bound. The highly realized rinpoches, such as the Dalai Lama and Kalu Rinpoche, tend to treat women students with respect and they're willing to abandon some arguably sexist traditions. The example Drolma offers from her own experience is that when she was in the Himalayas there were certain sacred rooms where women weren't supposed to go. But the high masters simply said, "Oh, you can come in," and they allowed women to live in the monasteries and study.

Drolma is grateful for all the support she has received from her male teachers, but in her opinion, women also need women role models; that is, they need to have women teachers and – even more importantly – to see that there are women who are highly realized. "My generation," says Drolma, "found women role models in history, and sometimes in the flesh, but that was rare." For women to really feel that it's possible for them to attain deep realization in this life, they need to know that there are women who have awakened before them.

The Buddha asserted that there is neither male nor female, and ultimately this is true. Yet on the ground – at the relative level – there *are* women and there *are* men. Beyond just having different bodies, we are socialized differently and accorded different roles and privileges. In a myriad of ways these factors determine how we experience the world and by extension how we experience the spiritual path. So, while both male and female teachers can speak on the universal human experience, women can also have a unique perspective that can be helpful to both male and female students. That's not to say that women teachers are better than male teachers or vice versa. There are simply different ways of expressing the dharma.

Recently, a man approached Drolma after hearing her teach. He was full of emotion. After years of studying Buddhism with male teachers, he was deeply touched by her unique expression of the dharma. She had helped him to finally understand the very heart of the tradition.

6060

Any Last Thoughts?

A Q&A with Simon Critchley

Maybe your Philosophy-101 textbook was dry as a bone and your philosophy class (MWF 11 a.m.–12 p.m.) was a good opportunity to doze. But don't hold that against Simon Critchley. Though he's a professor and chair of philosophy at the New School for Social Research in New York, he's not like the prof you had. His latest book, *The Book of Dead Philosophers*, unpacks three thousand years of philosophical history by explaining how "190 or so" philosophers have kicked off. And this, surprisingly, is a lively read – life affirming and morbidly funny.

Why a book on dead philosophers?

Philosophy began with a death. Socrates walked around Athens asking questions no one had ever asked before. Difficult, universal questions about the nature of things: What is justice? Beauty? Truth? People answered Socrates' questions and he picked apart their answers, but he didn't provide answers himself, just a series of perplexities. For that he was executed by the authorities. The philosopher always has his or her eyes on death. Focused on questions of finitude, he's already in a sense half dead himself. To philosophize is to learn how to die in the right way, at the right time. This is what the philosophical tradition keeps coming back to.

Is there such thing as a good death?

I think so. Dignity is key. Most people now die in a drug-induced state, and in some cases, this interferes with dignity. In the past, a lot of people died in pain, but that wasn't necessarily bad. A great example is Epicurus. He died in enormous pain, yet he endured and died with tranquility. This was essential to his teaching: do not fear death.

These days, the overwhelming issue is not dying in pain, not being a burden to anybody else. So, there's a sense that you should drug people, pacify them. Yet there are people in the modern age who have done other things – Freud, for instance. He had twenty-seven operations for cancer of the mouth and refused to take painkillers because, he said, he'd rather think in pain than not think at all.

How else has the culture of death changed over time?

In the past, deaths were often group acts – the dying were surrounded by friends. And death was something that was meditated on throughout life. It wasn't something one tried to run away from. Our culture denies death in a dramatic way, particularly in the U.S., where most people have never even seen a corpse. Looking at the history of the philosophical death can get people to look at the skull beneath the skin – to focus on the one certainty in life, apart from taxes, which is that life ends.

Has any other society denied death to the extent we do?

Societies have denied death in different ways, but we're so extreme it's difficult to think of a precedent. We shuffle dying off as something that happens to other people, not to us. We see death as obscene. The Victorians had difficulties with sex but they had a powerful death culture and were very good at commemorating it. We're the opposite. We can talk about sex until we're blue in the face but we cannot face death. We're terrified of it. This is strange in an overwhelmingly Christian culture, because Christianity is a meditation on death. It's about learning to die in a certain way. Longevity wasn't something of much value in early Christianity – a brief life was often a worthier life.

The denial of death is the overwhelming desire for longevity at all costs, and the gods people believe in are the gods of medical technology. I'm not against that but we should be thinking about the issue more carefully.

What about the classical Chinese philosophy of death?

Confucianism was all about the right manners and the right behavior, so the Confucians were obsessed with rituals around death. Daoists rejected that, thinking death was a passage from one state to another: we're human beings, we become worm food, and then we might become something else. Who knows? The Daoist Chuang Tzu laughed and banged on a tub after his wife died, saying, "My wife has left me." Then a friend said, "How can you possibly laugh when your wife is dead?" "We lived together," Chuang Tzu said, "We had children. We had a wonderful time. Now she has transformed. Why should I be sad?" The Confucians were appalled by this because it seemed to show no respect for the dead.

Tell me about Japanese death poems.

On the verge of death, Zen monks write a haiku or short elegiac poem. They pronounce it, and then set aside their ink brush, cross their arms, straighten their back, and die – often in the meditative position. It's pretty impressive [laughs]. An example of one of these poems is "the joy of dew drops in the grass as they turn back to vapor." There's a wonderful story of a Zen Buddhist monk from the twelfth century who preached to his disciples and then sat in the Zen position and died. When his followers complained he died too quickly, he revived and harangued them for a bit longer. Then he died five days later. This was about controlling the moment of his death.

Which philosopher's death appeals to you most?

I like Wittgenstein's. He was diagnosed with cancer a month or two before he died and he treated the news with great relief. He then moved in with his doctor and struck up a firm friendship with his doctor's wife, Mrs. Bevan – going to the pub with her every night. He died the day after his birthday, but on his birthday, Mrs. Bevan gave him an electric blanket and she said, "Many happy returns." Then Wittgenstein said, "There will be no return." There's something sober and funny about that, which I think is important. It's important to maintain a certain lightness toward death. To face up to it and replace the terror with sober humor.

You wrote another book called On Humor. *What's the connection for you between philosophy and comedy?*

Philosophy asks you to look at the world as if you were from another planet and to question everything – the nature of reality, the external world, other people. That's like comedy – great comedy, not the dreary stand-up routines you usually see. At their best, both comedians and philosophers shake out your prejudices. Jokes can liberate and elevate us and even change the situation we find ourselves in.

We fear our own deaths, but there's also the problem of dealing with the deaths of loved ones. How do philosophers help us work with that?

Badly. The question of death was really posed for me through the death of my father and friends. But the philosopher's death is about *my* death and *me* dying calmly, with dignity. This doesn't get at the difficulty of our response to the death of those we love. That's why in *The Book of Dead Philosophers* I spend the time on early Christian philosophers – they had the best sense of grief. Now I'm working on a book about the nature of love, particularly the nature of mystical love. Philosophy has a lot of wisdom about what the world means, and that's fantastic, but it doesn't have a rich enough vocabulary for the question of love.

Awakening My Heart

My First Retreat with Thich Nhat Hanh

The War Memorial Gym is a sea of eight hundred prone people. When I finally find an empty patch of floor, I unfurl my
yoga mat. Then I lie down on top of it, covering myself with the
itchy yellow blanket I carted here from my dorm room.

This is the evening of the first full day of Thich Nhat
Hanh's Awakening the Heart Retreat, held in Vancouver at the
University of British Columbia. According to the schedule, we'll
be practicing total relaxation and touching the earth. I don't know
what touching the earth is, but I don't give it much thought. My
mind has latched onto the pleasant promise of total relaxation.
And it *is* pleasant. Sister Chan Khong, who has worked closely
with Thich Nhat Hanh for over fifty years, assures us that if we
feel like sleeping, we don't need to resist. Instead, we can enjoy drifting off and later waking up refreshed. She guides us in
breathing, releasing, and taking notice of the wonders of our
bodies – the hard work of our hearts, livers, intestines. Then she
breaks into soothing song.

When the bell finally rings and Sister Chan Khong moves
on to touching the earth, I am deeply relaxed. She explains that
we all have three roots: blood (or genetic) ancestors, environment (or land) ancestors, and spiritual ancestors. They are the
sources of our strength and goodness, but they also plant the
seeds of our pain and negative patterns. We're going to concentrate on the good seeds that are in us from each of our roots, and
then we're going to acknowledge the negative seeds. We're going
to touch the earth by touching the floor with our forehead, and
we're going to let this negativity go – let it go into the earth.
Sister Chan Khong also explains that she is going to talk about
different situations and maybe they won't all apply to us, but we

can use what she's saying as a jumping off point to think about our own lives.

We begin with our blood ancestors – first our mother. My own relationship with my mom is remarkably uncomplicated; she is a true friend and has been supportive of me all my life. So I don't relate when Sister Chan Khong talks about the challenges of having a critical, complaining mother. But when she tells us to imagine our mother when she was young, and to think about her vulnerability and her pain, I start crying instantly. It's like Sister Chan Khong has pressed a button I didn't know I had. I'm picturing my mother at age fourteen, when she lost her little brother in an accident. She washed his blood off the porch, she told me once, and she felt like she was washing him down the drain.

On the wall opposite me hangs the gym's scoreboard, flanked by the stylized heads of two thunderbirds. I close my eyes to them and let my tears drip to the pink foaminess of my yoga mat.

Then Sister Chan Khong tells us to think of our father.

Over breakfast when I was eleven, I asked my dad if he believed in ghosts. "See this coffeepot," he said, holding it up to the morning light. "I believe in this coffeepot because I can see it. I don't believe in what I can't see."

I bit into a corner of toast with jam. "So you think that when we die, that's it?"

"Not at all," he said. "We live on through our children."

I squinted at my father, still in his bathrobe, and decided that *living on through our children* was just a fancy-schmancy way of saying that when you're dead, you're dead. This was a no-frills belief I couldn't share, because I believed in most everything else – heaven and God, reincarnation and astral planes, ghosts, astrology, and psychic powers. With its many mysterious layers, my eleven-year-old world was both thrilling and terrifying. Attics held untold possibility; I slept with blankets over my head; I went to fortune-tellers. Be it palm readings, tea leaves, or tarot cards, witchy middle-aged women in slippers predicted great things for me. What they never predicted was doubt.

Yet after I left eleven behind – after years had gone by – my beliefs came to look more and more like Dad's. Pragmatic. Evidence-based. I was my father's daughter.

"You cannot take your father out of you; you cannot take your mother out of you," Thich Nhat Hanh says during a dharma talk in the War Memorial Gym. "You are a continuation of your father; you are a continuation of your mother. In fact, your father is both inside and outside. The father inside is younger, and you carry the inside father into the future."

Thich Nhat Hanh (known affectionately as Thay) is up on the stage, pots of orchids beside him. This, the first part of his talk, is dedicated to the children who are on the retreat, and they're sitting on the floor directly in front of the stage. I'm on the floor too, but further back, and behind me there are people on chairs.

"Bring a grain of corn home, plant it in a small pot, and remember to water it every day." Thich Nhat Hanh says. "Then when the grain of corn has become a young plant of corn of two or three leaves, ask the plant this question: My dear little plant of corn, do you remember the time when you were a tiny seed?"

Thay's smile is wide as he gives the children these instructions, and this gets everyone else smiling too – both children and adults. "If you listen very carefully, you can hear the answer," he says. "The young plant of corn will say something like: 'Me? A tiny seed? I don't believe it!'" A brown-robed Zen master cracking a silly joke – this gets people giggling.

"The young plant of corn has been there for only for two weeks," says Thay, "but it has already forgotten that it was a seed, a tiny seed of corn, so you have to help the plant to remember. Tell it something like this: 'My dear little plant of corn, it's me who planted the grain of corn in this pot and who has watered it every day. You came from that seed.' Maybe in the beginning the plant doesn't believe you, but be patient and it will accept that it was once a seed."

I am already familiar with Thich Nhat Hanh's grain of corn teaching – I've read it in his books – but it sounds fresh right now. He is delivering it as if he's never delivered it before, and I'm hearing it that way. Thay says that practitioners of meditation can see the grain of corn when they look at the plant – meditation allows them to do this. So maybe it is this retreat, with its meditation and mindfulness practices, which is allowing me to see more layers and live differently. Lots of little things feel different since the retreat started. Last night, for instance when I went back to my dorm, I unwrapped the vegan chocolate peanut butter brownie that I'd been too full to eat at lunch. I sat on my bed and just ate, concentrating on the soft, sweet frosting, the chewy nuttiness. Back in the non-retreat world, I never just eat; I'm in too much of a hurry for that. I read at the same time, or else I talk or tidy the kitchen. This slowed down life feels a lot better. It tastes better too.

"The grain of corn has not died," Thay continues. "You can no longer see the grain of corn, but you know that it has not died. If it had died, there would be no plant of corn. You cannot take the grain of corn out of the plant of corn.

"We are the continuation of our father and our mother, like the plant of corn is the continuation of the seed of corn," Thay told the children. "In the beginning, every one of us was much smaller even than the seed of corn. But we don't remember, so we need a friend in the dharma to remind us that we were once this very tiny seed in our mother's womb – half of the seed from our father and the other half from our mother. Your father is in every cell of your body; your mother is in every cell of your body. So when your father dies, he doesn't really die. He lives on in you, and you bring him into the future."

In October 2008, I had just fallen asleep at my grandmother's house when my aunt Peggy shook me awake. "No," I said, sitting bolt upright.

"Yes," she said. "Quick."

I was already dressed, so I threw off the covers and ran down the dark stairs after her. But I didn't understand: If *yes*, why this rush? Wasn't it over? Didn't death look like falling into sleep? I imagined the transition being like a kite disappearing into the sky. The kite would go higher and higher – deeper and deeper into dreams – then the cord tying it to earth would release, all the kite colors peacefully swallowed up in blue.

But no kites, no open sky – in the TV room turned hospice, my father was gasping, struggling to find air for his body swollen with cancer. There were five women gathered on and around his hospital bed – me, my two aunts, my grandmother, and my father's third wife – and each of us was shouting last minute messages to him. "Let go, Stephen," my aunt Valerie urged, making it sound like "push" in a delivery room. "There's nothing to worry about here."

The gasps got further and further apart and his eyes glazed. Aunt Peggy checked his pulse. "He's gone," she said.

It wasn't yet dawn; we had hours before the people from the funeral home would come with their black bag. So I stayed sitting on the hospital bed – between the wall and my father slowly going cold. I wanted to sob, but held back because I didn't want to make this more painful for my grandmother or the others. My grandmother, I was pretty sure, also wanted to sob, but held back for me and the others. Maybe this is how families always support each other: individuals keeping themselves glued together for the benefit of all. I talked quietly with cousins, aunts, and uncles.

"The people from the home will be here in half an hour," my aunt Peggy finally said, and my heart contracted. Sobbing I could do later, alone. What could only happen now was wedging myself into the crook of my father's arm. I tried to pull his elbow to the side, and it was like ice water in my face when I realized I couldn't – he'd gone stiff. Still I crawled between his arm and his chest – that small, rigid space just as it was – and there I breathed for both of us, following the breath.

This was a rare moment in my life – I had my father all to myself for half an hour.

"Some young people are angry with their father," Thich Nhat Hanh says. "They cannot talk to their father. There is hate." Then Thay tells us in his soft, accented voice about a young man he once knew who was so angry at his father that he wanted nothing to do with him.

The children, with their tiny, bare feet, are still in the gymnasium turned dharma hall with the adults, and I'm surprised by how quiet and attentive they are. Sitting by one of the loudspeakers is Alison, my retreat roommate, her hand on her baby-round belly.

"If you look deeply into the young man," continues Thay, "you will see that his father is fully present in every cell of his body and he cannot take his father out of him. So when you get angry with your father, you get angry with yourself. Suppose the plant of corn got angry at the grain of corn."

I've never been like the young man that Thay knew. My father and I were always on good terms, but – though I never told him this – it touched off seeds of anger in me when he got sick.

My father left when I was four. One day, my mother and I came home and there was a note on the kitchen table. There was also a plate with sandwich crusts on it – the leftovers of the lunch he'd eaten before getting on a plane to Calgary, a faraway city where a woman was waiting for him. I didn't see my father for two years. After that, I saw him for a couple of weeks every summer when I'd visit him and his new family. The nanny would feed me and my half-siblings dinner and then I'd get sent to bed at the same time as them. They were seven and nine years younger than me, so bedtime would come when it was still light and I'd stare at the ceiling, sleepless. Later, after Dad and his second wife started having problems, he stopped buying me plane tickets to Calgary. He visited me instead, and we played Trivial Pursuit and he took me out to practice my driving. I didn't feel, though, that he really came to see me. He stayed at his mother's place and spent most of the time drinking wine and moonshine with his siblings and cousins.

As I grew up, I inherited my father's skepticism but not the other pillar of his philosophy – the belief that we continue through our children. With a gulf so wide between us, I couldn't see myself as a continuation of him. Of course, I wasn't denying biology; I understood that fifty percent of my genetic information came from him. But so what? Genetics could explain my cleft chin, not who I was. After all, my father had another three children with his second wife and one more with his third, and all of us progeny were uniquely ourselves. One of my half-sisters was so angry with Dad that she refused to have contact with him.

According to Thay, if we're angry with our father or mother, we have to breathe in and out, and find reconciliation. This is the only path to happiness, and if we can live a happy, beautiful life, our father and mother in us will be more beautiful also. "During sitting meditation," says Thay, "I like to talk to my father inside. One day I told him, 'Daddy, we have succeeded.' That morning, when I practiced, I felt that I was so free, so light, I did not have any desire, any craving. I wanted to share that with my father, so I talked to my father inside: 'Daddy, we are free.'"

"I also talk to my mother," continues Thay, "because I know that my mother has not really died – she continues on in me. When I practiced walking meditation in India with a group of a few thousand people on the largest boulevard of New Delhi, I invited my mother to walk with me. I said, 'Mommy, let's walk together. Use my feet, but also yours. My feet are the continuation of your feet.' So, mother and son, we enjoyed walking in New Delhi. I invited also my father to walk with me. Then later on, I invited my brother and my grandmother and the Buddha and my teacher. The walk was so wonderful."

The university gym has a blue glow – blue floor, blue seats in the bleachers, closed blue curtains filtering the morning light. Thay has a glow too – a warm smile. "When we make a happy step, all our ancestors enjoy walking and making happy steps," he says. "If you walk in the Kingdom of God, all of them walk in the Kingdom of God. If you walk in Hell – in despair and anger and hate – your ancestors have to join you. Let us choose to walk in the Kingdom of God, in the Pure Land of the Buddha."

Interbeing: this is Thich Nhat Hanh's term for dependent origination, a key concept in Buddhism, which states that all phenomena arise together in a mutually interdependent web of cause and effect. In traditional Buddhist literature, this is a doctrine that can come across as philosophical and cerebral. Thich Nhat Hanh, however, has a gift for presenting Buddhist teachings in very human, very personal terms. At the retreat, he uses the orchids on the stage to explain interbeing. To exist a flower needs sun, clouds, rain, earth, minerals, and a gardener. Many non-flower elements come together to help the flower manifest and if we remove these non-flower elements, there is no flower left.

In a similar way, so-called opposites always manifest together, inseparably. There is no darkness without light, no left without right, no above without below, no parent without child. "Before the son or daughter manifests, you cannot call the father a father," Thay explains. "Of whom would he be the father?" In other words, my father and I inter-are. We all inter-are.

I used to believe that my father had no excuse for his behavior – his chronic infidelities, his willingness to abandon. After all, his own father, Buddy, wasn't like that. Buddy had probably never heard of Rev. Theodore M. Hesburgh, the longtime president of Notre Dame. Yet he lived Hesburgh's well-known quote: "The most important thing that a father can do for his children is to love their mother." The Awakening the Heart retreat is helping me to look more deeply into things. To see the rain in the flower or the piece of paper. To see that my father was a product of many causes and conditions.

Like me, like all of us, my father was wounded. I don't know the source of his suffering and maybe I never will. But I understand suffering. My father was trying to fill himself up with busyness, women, and booze. No one does that unless they hurt.

If Thich Nhat Hanh is right and my father is indeed in me, then I can heal his wounds. When I heal my wounds, it heals his, and it heals the wounds of future generations. With my suffering transformed, I won't pass it along. The cycle stops.

Touching the earth is the last activity of the evening, so afterward I fall into "noble" silence along with the other retreatants and I file out of the gym. It's a special feeling to walk without words with hundreds of people. Little sounds take on new texture. There's the sound of feet on hard concrete, then the sound of feet on softer earth, rustling through grass. Thich Nhat Hanh has taught us to do walking meditation at a normal clip. In this way, we can do it always, anywhere. Inhale, I take three steps; exhale, five. Inhale. Exhale.

The Douglas firs tower darkly above me, and a weeping silver linden gives off its perfume. Roots, branches, leaves – I feel my connection to these trees, the way that they take in my breath and the breath of all of us, and then give it back to us as oxygen. I feel connected to the other retreatants, too, united in our practice, in our inhalations and exhalations. And I feel connected to my father. I have a debt to him – a debt for this life. I used to believe my father left me twice – once to be with his second wife and once to die. But he didn't leave at all. Thay's right – my father is walking with me now.

In the Country of the Present Moment

My Second Retreat with Thich Nhat Hanh

I thought there would be a brown-robed monk or nun to pick me up at the train station. Instead, there was a Parisian with closely clipped hair, piercings, and red clam diggers. Together we heaved my suitcase into the van. Then we fumbled in English and French, as she sped full throttle along country roads bathed in the buttery last light of day. We passed an orchard of plum trees, quaintly shuttered stone homes, and tidy rows of grape vines. Yet what cut through my two-plane, three-train jet lag was the fields of sunflowers. Their green stalks and leaves, yellow petals, and brown centers were an image I'd so often seen in literature on Plum Village. I knew I was finally arriving.

Zen master Thich Nhat Hanh calls Plum Village "the country of the present moment." Located in southwestern France, it is the full-time home of some two hundred monastics and annually welcomes thousands of retreatants from across the globe. Nuns, monks, lay practitioners – for thirty years they've been putting into practice Thich Nhat Hanh's teachings on community and enlightened society. But, day by day, breath by breath, *how* are they living the teachings? And what, ultimately, are the tools they're discovering that we could all use to transform our lives, no matter where we are? In making my pilgrimage to Plum Village, these are the questions I wanted to explore.

According to Thich Nhat Hanh, or Thay as he is affectionately called by his students, the essence of his teachings is twofold. One, how you can learn to handle – not cover up – your painful, strong emotions and, two, how to bring joy and happiness into your life. "You can be happy here and now," he told me. "You don't have to look for happiness elsewhere."

"Mindfulness is a kind of energy that you can produce," Thay continued. "It's the energy that helps bring your mind back to your body, so you can live your life more deeply. Mindfulness is the energy that allows you to be aware of what is going on with your body, your feelings, your perceptions – to know what's going on in you and around you. When you drink tea in mindfulness, you are truly there. You are in touch with the tea; you are truly in the here and the now. But if you are possessed by worry, if you think a lot about the past and the future, then the tea is not truly there. There is no real life. It's like a dream."

With mindfulness, Thay said, "you can touch the nature of inter-being. Once you get that insight, discrimination and fear vanish. You know that your happiness is the happiness of other people. Their sorrow is your sorrow. Everything inter-is with everything else."

On the morning of my first day at Plum Village, it was still dark when I woke to the sound of a young sister ringing a bell, signaling that it was time to get ready for meditation. My dorm was in Hillside, an old farmhouse in New Hamlet, a section of the center that houses nuns, lay single women, and families. All Plum Village retreatants are part of a dharma family who eat and do chores together and have almost daily group discussions. My dharma family was made up of the retreatants staying at Hillside and because our designated chore was washing up after meals, we were known as the Joyful Scrubbers.

The head of my dharma family was Sister Loving-Kindness who had been a nurse for twenty years before ordaining in 1991. "Thay has created Plum Village with the wish that we use the family as a model for relationships," she told me. "We have elder brothers, elder sisters, younger brothers, younger sisters. The sangha is our support, our home, and a resource for us throughout our practice life. Even if there's temporary conflict within a small segment of the community, there are others to embrace the two people who may be having difficulties. That's the benefit of practicing with a community."

Thay, in his first dharma talk of the week, expanded on the importance of sangha. "It's possible to practice alone, as individuals," he said. "But you might lose your practice after a few months because you don't have a sangha to guide you, to protect you, to support you. That's why a good practitioner always tries to build a sangha in his town or village. Even a buddha needs a sangha."

If we are merely individual drops of water, we will evaporate on our way to the ocean. To arrive at the ocean, we must go as a river, as a community. "Go like a river," said Thay. "Allow the river to embrace you. If you allow the collective energy of the sangha to penetrate into your heart and help hold your suffering, you will suffer less in just a few minutes."

My interview with Thich Nhat Hanh took place on No Car Day, the day each week that everyone at Plum Village limits their carbon footprint by not driving. In a small, simple room, he was stretched out on a green hammock, drinking oolong from a clear cup and nibbling on candied ginger. Clustered around him were several nuns, and Thay introduced one of them to me as his attendant – a young sister from Indonesia. Then he invited her to sing an Indonesian children's song, which, if I understood correctly, told a sweet tale about a parrot.

I flicked on my recorder. "Should we start?" I asked.

"Should we start what?" Thay joked. "Sitting on a hammock?" It was a gentle reminder that – though my nerves may have been jangled because I felt I was in the presence of a special, important person – Thay was not making a big deal out of himself. Despite being nominated for the Nobel Peace Prize by Martin Luther King, Jr., despite penning more than one hundred books, despite all his remarkable achievements, Thay wears brown – as do all the monastics in his lineage – because that's the color the peasants in his Vietnamese homeland have traditionally worn. He is of the people.

A bell rang in the distance. "I'm mindful of the bell," Thay said. "While I listen to the bell, I don't think. I concentrate on my breath and on the sound of the bell. When you are mindful of something, you are concentrated on it, and the power of mindful concentration can help you see things as they really are and you discover the nature of inter-being."

Thay is well known for coining the term "inter-being," which refers to the interconnectedness of all things. Over the years, he has frequently used the image of a flower to explain this teaching. Sunflower, orchid, lotus – if you are mindful and concentrated, you can see that a flower is made of infinite non-flower elements. A flower is made up of not just rain but also the cloud that released the rain. It's made up of not just soil but also the decomposed plants and animals that enrich the soil. If you re-move any of the non-flower elements from the flower, the flower ceases to exist. "So the flower cannot exist alone," Thay told me. "It has to inter-be with everything else in the cosmos." The same is true of people. "A human being is made of non-human ele-ments, and if you remove the non-human elements, the human being is no longer there. So a human cannot be by herself alone. She has to inter-be with everything else in the cosmos."

According to Thich Nhat Hanh, our insight into inter-being is the key to our happiness. "Suffering and happiness inter-are," he said. "If you understand suffering deeply, you know how to make good use of suffering in order to produce happiness. You know that happiness is made of non-happiness elements, and one of these non-happiness elements is suffering. So suffering has a role in making happiness possible.

"It's like the lotus and the mud. Without mud, you cannot grow a lotus. Without the mud of suffering, you cannot create happiness. This is why, if you touch the nature of inter-being, you don't try to run away from suffering anymore. Instead you try to embrace your suffering. You look deeply into it to under-stand its nature and to learn how to make good use of suffering to produce happiness."

"If you have gone through a war," Thay continued, "you have the capacity to appreciate the peace that's available in the here and now. Many people do not appreciate peace until a war breaks out. But against the background of suffering, you appreciate the peace that's available." Likewise, when a person is healthy, he may not appreciate his health. But when he falls sick, he regrets that he did not fully enjoy being healthy and then, when he gets better, he does fully enjoy it. "So, suffering and happiness inter-are. They are like left and right, above and below, the mud and the lotus. The understanding of inter-being removes all discrimination – all dualistic thinking – and creates harmony, understanding, and peace. The practice of mindfulness has the purpose of bringing you the insight of inter-being."

For a concrete method of practicing mindfulness in daily life, Thich Nhat Hanh has crafted the Five Mindfulness Trainings, a modern take on the five precepts. These trainings are (1) reverence for life, (2) true happiness, (3) true love, (4) loving speech and deep listening, and (5) nourishment and healing. "The Five Mindfulness Trainings are based on the insight of inter-being," Thay told me. "The insight of inter-being is the ground of better ethics. Then the five trainings are applied ethics that can help reduce suffering and bring more happiness."

In his book *Good Citizens*, Thay wrote, "The Five Mindfulness Trainings are offered without dogma or religion. Everybody can use them as an ethics for their life without becoming Buddhist or becoming part of any tradition or faith. You are just yourself, but you try to make a beautiful life by following these guidelines." Following the trainings, he wrote, "leads to healing, transformation, and happiness for ourselves and for the world."

1. Reverence for Life

While at Plum Village, I shared meals with my dharma family under a tree hung with a swing set. There were more than twenty of us, and we didn't start eating until we were all seated and we'd taken a moment to contemplate our food as a gift from the earth, the sky, farmers, packers, deliverers, and cooks. Then the bell rang and we took our first bites, silently. In order for us to more fully appreciate what was on our plate, there was no talking as we ate. Just the tiny clinking of forks, knives, spoons.

Many people report that, at first, they find it awkward to eat in silence. But for me, right away it was a relief. Normally I eat with the TV on or with a book in my hand or while talking. Normally, I think this two-things-at-once eating will relax me. Maybe it does a little, but not like eating in silence with my dharma family. In the quiet, I could actually concentrate on the flavors and textures and origins of each mouthful.

Steaming bowls of soup with a clear broth, delicate rice noodles, and chewy mushrooms; bread pudding made from hunks of baguette, mashed bananas, and dark chocolate; pasta salad punctuated with the salty punch of wrinkled black olives. All the food at Plum Village is vegan, reflecting the first mindfulness training, reverence for life. Like many Plum Village practitioners, when I pay attention to what I eat, I don't want to eat flesh – to eat the suffering of animals.

Sister Jewel, who grew up in Chicago and Nairobi, talked to me about the subtleties of reverence for life. "We inter-are with everything, so if we harm anything we're harming ourselves," she said. "If we see that deeply, then we can only practice reverence for life – for all of life."

At Plum Village, the sangha takes every opportunity to guide people toward reconciliation, peace, and non-violence. This includes hosting retreats for Israelis and Palestinians. To begin, the Israelis and Palestinians separately learn to relax and get in touch with their feelings, their suffering. Then, after a week of experiencing the safety of their own group and the peaceful, loving environment of Plum Village, the Israelis and Palestinians come together for conversation, during which they learn that the other group has also suffered. Previously, according to Sister Jewel, "they saw each other as the enemy, but when they really talk and listen to each other, they see that they have a lot in common." After experiencing a retreat at Plum Village, many Israelis and Palestinians are inspired to work for peace and reconciliation between the two communities.

"We emphasize sangha living because if you have that kind of solid foundation for your life, you will be a peacemaker," said Sister Jewel. "You will be someone who doesn't contribute to violence and who protects life. Protecting life – loving life – starts with loving the life in ourselves and not discriminating against our own suffering, our own pain. When we don't discriminate against the ugly things or the painful things in us, then we also learn not to discriminate against people who we believe are not very kind, not very wholesome. Discrimination is the root of the destruction of life. When we think that something is not okay, when we believe that 'This is me and that's not me,' that discrimination is the root that gives rise to the mind of killing and destruction." At Plum Village, Sister Jewel concluded, "We get to the root of discrimination through the understanding of inter-being."

2. True Happiness

"True happiness is not made of fame, power, wealth, or sensual pleasure, but rather of understanding and love," Thich Nhat Hanh said during our interview. "The capacity to live in the here and the now allows you to recognize that you already have everything you need to be happy. You don't need to run into the future to look for happiness."

At Plum Village, none of the monastics has a personal bank account or car or computer. None even has a personal email address. For a monastic, Sister Clarity told me, "there is nothing personal – we share everything from our living space to our ideas. We live in rooms with three, four, or five sisters or brothers together. Last winter, I stayed in a room with the largest number of us. There were seven."

Yet living without the stuff of normal lay life doesn't create unhappiness. Interviewing Sister Clarity in the New Hamlet bookshop, I knew she was happy even before I asked – her smiles were that wide and frequent. But growing up the youngest of seven children, she's used to living in community and it's what she values.

"Right now, I'm sharing a room with two other sisters," Sister Clarity said. "I take care of one sister and she takes care of the other sister and, in turn, that last sister takes care of me." This, she continued, "is what we call having a second body. We look out for each other, not just in terms of health but also in terms of each other's well-being and practice. That's the nice thing about living together. We have a chance to build sisterhood."

I mulled that over. It did sound like a beautiful practice, but I was stuck on the idea of having – at the very least – a personal email account.

Sister Clarity smiled. "It's nice not having your own email or bank account," she said. "It's nice because it's one less thing to worry about."

3. True Love

On Lazy Day, a day at Plum Village without a formal schedule, I attended a wedding. It began with walking meditation. The nuns were in front wearing their conical hats and brown robes. Then the couple walked behind them, followed by the guests. Slowly and silently, we wound our way between New Hamlet's curly-roofed bell tower and bamboo grove and all around the large lotus pond before arriving at the Full Moon Meditation Hall. Inside, the couple sat before the altar on their purple zabutons – the bride's white dress ballooning around her and the groom in his suit and socks.

They had been together for seven years, and the vows they made to each other reflected their intimacy. Ian thanked Raphaelle for introducing him to the Plum Village community and for the multitude of good things she'd brought to his life, saying that without her support he would never have produced his first music album. He promised to water her good seeds by giving her the compliments she well deserved and to do his share of the housework. In her turn, Raphaelle expressed her appreciation for the way Ian made her feel, including when she felt shy or insecure. "You're a good practitioner," she told him. "I know you'll remind me to go back to my breath when I need to calm down, and I will support you when you feel stressed by giving you space to go back to the present moment."

True love, the third mindfulness training, is about making a deep, long-term commitment to a partner, like the one Ian and Raphaelle were declaring that day. It is not a heavy-handed law forbidding sex outside of marriage, nor is it a list of appropriate sexual acts or a judgment regarding sexual orientation. Instead, this training declares that the proper context for sexual relations is a serious commitment made known to one's family and friends.

While at Plum Village, I spoke with Will Stephens, who for several years has been attending the summer retreat with his family. "Through this practice," said Stephens, "I'm beginning to learn what true love actually is." It is not, he explained, "*I love you if you meet my needs.*" It's about helping the person you love to be free and happy. "I believe I wouldn't be with my wife now without this practice. I wouldn't have had the clarity to see it wasn't my wife that was the problem. It was my own problem."

In this post-'60s world, Stephens said, people find it difficult to embrace the training of true love because they like to be able to have sexual relationships without committing long-term. "But in my experience, damage is done to myself and the other person if we have that level of intimacy without commitment. It's an intrusion into that person's and my own psyche."

"I had the experience of sexual relations outside of my marriage," Stephens admitted, "and that caused a lot of pain to myself, my wife, and the other person." It's important to remember that sexual desire is not love, and sometimes cravings for sex actually stem from a deeper need to connect or to validate the self. "For me," said Stephens, "sexual desire has often been motivated by loneliness, so when my relationship has not been strong, my loneliness has been intense." But, as the third mindfulness training states, "Sexual activity motivated by craving always harms myself as well as others." It can only ever be a band-aid to loneliness.

Living true love isn't easy, Stephens acknowledges. "We have to work at it." The real key is "taking care of the true love, so that the sexual commitment takes care of itself." These days, he and his wife regularly take time to appreciate each other and to communicate any hurt or difficult emotions that they're experiencing. Now there's a lot of love in the relationship; there's fidelity.

The wedding at Plum Village ended with hugging meditation – the bride and groom in each other's arms for a long time. Then, outside the meditation hall, they smiled as the guests showered them in flower petals.

4. Loving Speech and Deep Listening

Sister Chan Khong has been working side by side with Thich Nhat Hanh for more than fifty years and is recognized as a major force in the development of Plum Village. She's also a gifted teacher and, during the retreat, she came to New Hamlet one afternoon to teach a practice called Beginning Anew. It's a practice that supports the mindfulness training of loving speech and deep listening.

A four-step process, Beginning Anew involves looking deeply and honestly at yourself and improving your relationships through mindful communication. The first step is to express appreciation for the person you're speaking to, so that you "water his or her good seeds." That is, you draw attention to their positive qualities and thereby help those qualities grow stronger. Now for the second step: acknowledging any unskillful action you've committed in your interactions with the other person. For this, mindfulness can help because it hones your awareness. Next, the third step is to reveal how the other person has hurt you. Here it's crucial to express yourself in a loving way, without blame – you don't want to make the other person defensive but rather encourage him or her to openly explain their behavior. Finally, the fourth step is to share any difficulty that you're experiencing and request support. After that, the person speaking and the person listening can change roles.

At Plum Village, the monastic community practices the first two steps of Beginning Anew collectively every other week and practices the full four steps in pairs or small groups whenever there's a need. Sister Chan Khong urges laypeople to practice Beginning Anew at home. It's even possible to practice Beginning Anew when the person you're speaking with has never heard of the practice. You can informally go through the steps without the expectation that the other person will reciprocate, and – according to Sister Chan Khong – over time the person's attitude toward you will shift for the better.

As she said to the group at New Hamlet, "When you look at me, you have a perception of Sister Chan Khong, but your perception is only five or ten percent of the reality. The same is true when you look at the person you've just fallen in love with or at the person you think you hate." Our perceptions are imperfect, and in order to understand others more, we need to communicate with them.

5. Nourishment and Healing

A mulberry tree by three Buddha statues was arrayed with little pieces of colored paper cut into the shapes of hearts, flowers, candles. From my knapsack, I fished out my own little piece of lime-green paper and wrote on it the names of the family I'd lost so far in my life – grandfathers, grandmother, father, uncle, and aunt. Then I taped the paper to a branch. Today at Plum

Village we were having a celebration to honor our ancestors and recognize that we're a continuation of them. The festivities included a picnic lunch with cake and Chinese dragons flapping their eyelids, wriggling their rumps, and leaping to the quick beat of a drum. What the festivities did *not* include was alcohol.

While it may be true that *I* can drink in moderation without any personal damage beyond a hangover, many people cannot. My children, my friends, my co-workers – I can't see into the double helix of their genes or into the secret corners of their frailties. In short, I can't know the harm alcohol could cause them in the future. But, by drinking with them and in front of them, I encourage their consumption. So the idea at Plum Village is that if we refrain from intoxicants, it's not for our own benefit alone.

In my interview with Sister Jewel, she talked to me about the Buddha's teachings on the four kinds of nutriments, which the fifth mindfulness training addresses. Beyond literal food and drink, there are sense impressions, volition, and consciousness. Sense impressions constitute the food we take in through our eyes and ears – the advertisements, films, books, and conversations we consume.

Volition, on the other hand, is what motivates us in our life; it's our aspiration. "If you want to become famous or make a lot of money, that wish is a kind of food," Sister Jewel explained. "It gives you energy to stay up late and sacrifice, but you can also have the motivation to relieve suffering, and that can also give you a lot of energy."

Finally, consciousness, the final nutriment, is what we "eat" all the time. According to Sister Jewel, "It comes from our own individual consciousness, our thoughts, our memories, and also the collective consciousness. If we're around people who have a lot of fear and anger, we're eating the collective-consciousness food of fear and anger. But if we're around people who are peaceful, that peace is a kind of food."

At Plum Village, practitioners try to mindfully consume each of these four kinds of nutriments. In terms of edible foods, said Sister Jewel, "We take only as much as we can eat, and we're grateful that we have something to nourish us to continue our practice." Regarding sense impressions, "We don't watch TV or listen to the radio or read the newspaper. We might go online to read, but we only take in what we need to know about what's happening in the world. We don't constantly consume news because the news is not the only reality. A lot of it is just focused on what's negative because that's what sells." If we consume so much news that we become depressed or apathetic, it doesn't help the global situation.

At Plum Village, the computers have bells, which occasionally ring to remind the user to breathe in and out. "Mindfulness bells are a kind of sense food that remind us to take care of ourselves and to not just be in the stream of our thinking the whole day," Sister Jewel explained. "Our thoughts are sometimes not such healthy food, so to stop the stream of thinking and get in touch with what's right here and now is nourishing. If we're attentive, we can hear the wind in the trees and the birds singing. There are so many things to be nourished by if we are aware.

"The collective consciousness food at Plum Village is very healthy, because there are two hundred monastics who are practicing mindfulness all day long, all year round. Plus, this week there are a thousand people here, and when you have a thousand people doing walking meditation together and eating mindfully together in dharma families, it's very powerful. It's very healing."

"The five mindfulness trainings are not laws or commandments," said Sister Peace, a nun who worked for the mayor of Washington, D.C., before ordaining. Some people decide not to take the trainings because they feel they'd have to do them just right. "Well, who of us can do anything perfectly?" Sister Peace asked. "The five mindfulness trainings are a direction in which we go. It's like the North Star is over there, so I'm going to go in that direction. And the farther I walk in that direction and transform, the clearer the path becomes.

"We can take many paths, but the essence – the summit – is mindfulness, truth, concentration, insight. Some people may follow the trainings much more strictly and some may just follow them in certain aspects. The key is to do whatever you do with awareness and mindfulness, because the more you become aware of what, for instance, eating meat or drinking wine does to you and your body, the more you can make an informed decision about whether you want to continue."

On my last evening at Plum Village, a ceremony for the five mindfulness trainings took place at the Full Moon Meditation Hall. In the center of the hall, facing the altar decked in fruit and flowers, sat the people who were taking the trainings, and I joined them there on a purple zabuton, even though I'd already taken the trainings the year before. Sister Peace is right that none of us can ever do anything perfectly, but breath by breath, moment by moment, we all have the capacity to live the trainings a little more fully. They are aspirations we can always renew.

Renewed, I filed out of the meditation hall with my dharma family. Then, as I was on my way back to Hillside for the last time, I realized I wasn't wearing my watch anymore – a watch with a face that said, in Thay's calligraphic script, *It's* in the middle and *now* at twelve, three, six, and nine o'clock. *It's now It's now It's now* ... always. I traced my steps back but couldn't find the watch and, with the sun going down, I felt sad because that watch was a little piece of Plum Village that I'd no longer be carrying home with me. Then I thought of Thay and my interview with him.

"Plum Village is not so much a place that is situated in time or space," he'd told me. "You can have it anywhere at any time. If you come to Plum Village and you don't know how to be in the present moment, it is not the country of the present moment. But if you are in America, or in Asia, and if you are in the present moment, you are in Plum Village. When you fly back to America, you can have Plum Village on the plane. You don't have to look for the future; you do not need to be caught in the past. If you know how to spend time with joy and peace, you are in Plum Village. You are in the country of the present moment."

The Tears I Shed Yesterday Have Become Rain

My Third Retreat with Thich Nhat Hanh

Zen master Thich Nhat Hanh has a soft, feathery voice. It is, we are informed, twenty decibels lower than average, so even when he's using a microphone, we must be perfectly quiet in order to hear him.

"It was fifty years ago on this very day," he nearly whispers, "that Martin Luther King gave a famous speech with the title 'I Have a Dream.'" Thich Nhat Hanh, or Thay, as he is affectionately known, pauses. "From time to time," he says with a smile, "I have a nice dream also."

This is the beginning of today's dharma talk, and the beginning is always my favorite. It's addressed especially to the children. From the toddler who likes to yodel during silent meals to the woman sitting in front of me with the pure-grey ponytail, there are more than eight hundred people on this six-day retreat. We are at Blue Cliff Monastery in Pine Bush, New York, and the theme we're exploring is "Transformation at the Base: The Art of Suffering." In other words, it's the very essence of the Buddhist path. Suffering is the inevitable common denominator of life. Buddhist practice transforms it into happiness and liberation.

"I'll tell you one of my dreams," Thay continues. "I had it about twenty years ago, when I was very young." The eighty-six-year-old monk smiles at the quiet joke he's cracking. "I was something like sixty-six. Very young."

Yet in his dream, he was even younger, maybe twenty-one or twenty-two, and he was overjoyed because he'd been accepted into the class of his university's best professor, a man who everyone said was exceptionally wise and kind. But on his way to the classroom for the first time, Thay saw a young man who looked exactly like him. He knew this young man was no other than himself and he wondered if the other him had also been accepted into the prestigious class. He stopped by the administration office to ask.

"No, no, not him," declared the lady in the office. "You, yes, but not him."

Thay left the office confused and grew more so when he learned that the illustrious professor was a professor of music. Not being a music student, Thay couldn't understand why he'd been accepted into this advanced class. Then he opened the class-room door, and inside there were over a thousand students, and the view through the window looked like Tusita Heaven – all waterfalls and mountain peaks covered with snow.

Surprise after surprise, Thay was informed that he had to give a music presentation as soon as the professor arrived. What was he going to do? Looking around for a solution, he put his hand in his pocket and felt the bowl of a small bell. Because he was a monk, the bell was the one instrument he was a master of, so with a happy heart, he waited for the professor's arrival. "He's coming, he's coming," Thay was told, but he never did get a glimpse of the professor. In that moment, Thay woke up.

"I stayed very still in my bed," he tells the Blue Cliff re-treatants, "and I tried to figure out what the dream meant." Thay realized that the young man who looked exactly like him was a self that he had left behind.

"Because I'd made efforts to practice," he says, "I overtook myself. That is why I was accepted, and he was not. In the pro-cess of practice, you become your better self with more freedom, more happiness."

The music class, according to Thay, symbolized an assembly of advanced Buddhist practitioners, while the professor symbol-ized the Buddha himself. "I regret that I did not have a few more minutes in the dream," Thay quips. "If I had, then I would have seen the Buddha in person."

During the Vietnam War, Thich Nhat Hanh was sleeping when a grenade was hurled through his window. He would have died, but it hit a curtain and ricocheted, exploding into the next room. On another occasion, grenades were thrown into the dormitories of the School of Youth for Social Service, an innovative grassroots organization he founded to improve education, sanitation, and farming practices in poor, rural communities. These grenades left two volunteers dead, a young man paralyzed, and a young woman riddled with a thousand pieces of shrapnel.

Thay and those working with him did not take sides in the war. No matter what the political allegiance of a victim, they would help him or her, and for this they were persecuted by the Vietnamese government and communists alike.

On June 1, 1965, Thich Nhat Hanh wrote a letter to Martin Luther King, Jr. in which he compared the struggle for peace in Vietnam to the civil rights movement in America and explained why some Vietnamese monastics felt driven to self-immolate. Now, half a century later, Thay offers that same explanation in the quiet of the Catskills.

"Both warring parties wanted to fight to the end, and we were caught in the middle," he says. "We wanted an end to the hostilities, but we did not have magazines, radio, or television, so our voice was lost in the bombs. That is why, in order to get the message across, we sometimes had to burn ourselves alive. Self-immolation was not an act of violence. It was an act of sacrifice in order to awaken the world to the suffering of the people in Vietnam."

One year after writing this letter, Thay was traveling across the United States to spread his urgent message of peace and, while in Chicago, he met Martin Luther King for the first time. Subsequently, King came out publicly against the war and nominated Thich Nhat Hanh for the Nobel Peace Prize, claiming that he knew no one worthier than "this gentle monk."

Later they saw each other again in Geneva, where they were both attending a peace conference. "I was able to tell him that the people in Vietnam admired him and called him a bodhisattva, a great being," says Thay. "He was pleased to hear that. We also discussed sangha building. The expression for sangha that he used was 'beloved community.'

"That was our last meeting before he got killed. When he was assassinated, I was in New York. I was angry and got sick. But I told myself I had to continue. I vowed that I would continue the work of sangha building."

Community is crucial, according to Thich Nhat Hanh, because without it no one can accomplish much. Even the Buddha needed a sangha, and the first thing he did when he got up from under the Bodhi tree was to establish one. Thich Nhat Hanh, however, found himself abruptly cut off from his sangha. After speaking out for peace, he was exiled from Vietnam and it would be almost forty years before he could return. "I was like a bee without a beehive," he says, "like a cell taken out of the body. I knew that if I did not practice well, then I would dry up."

He took political asylum in France and began gathering some friends around him. In the beginning, the sangha was so small that they had nowhere of their own to practice and had to ask the Quakers for the use of their space. Now Thich Nhat Hanh's sangha includes hundreds of monastics and tens of thousands of lay practitioners, with communities everywhere from Argentina to Austria, Botswana to Brazil.

I look around at the sangha in the Great Togetherness Meditation Hall at Blue Cliff. A week ago, I knew almost none of these retreatants, but now I know these painful facts: There's a man here whose son was killed in Sandy Hook Elementary School and another whose marriage is crumbling. There's a woman whose father is ill and another whose daughter died of leukemia.

There is suffering. That is the first noble truth. There is per-sonal suffering; there is societal suffering; and there is the tragic place where personal and societal suffering meet. But in commu-nity all of our suffering – in being heard and held – can soften, just a little.

"You are part of my sangha," Thay says to all of us.

The retreatants at Blue Cliff are divided into dharma fami-lies, small groups named after birds, trees, flowers. As families, we come together for mindful work and dharma discussion. When Willow, my family, gathers to talk, we always begin by giving each other our internal weather reports. Today, after we delve into our sunny skies, soft fogs, and snowstorms, Peggy Smith, one of our dharma discussion leaders, holds out a singing bowl. "Does anyone want to invite the bell?" she asks.

Peggy likes that in this tradition the bell is invited, never struck. She likes this careful, nonviolent attention to language. Step-by-step, we go through the ceremony for inviting the bell.

First, bring your palms together and bow. Next, place the bell in the center of your palm, thinking of your hand as a lotus flower and your fingers as its five petals. If you close your fingers around the bell, its sound will be stifled, so keep them open, fully bloomed. In and out, take two breaths. Then with the bell inviter – the little stick – gently tap the edge of the bell. This half ring is called "waking the bell" and it lets those around you know that soon there will be a full ring. This is an opportunity for everyone to stop what they're doing and simply enjoy the moment. Follow your breath for another eight seconds, or ten if you're generous. Then invite the bell fully. The sound, as Thay describes it, should be like a bird soaring up. Take three deep breaths and invite the bell again. And again – three breaths and one final invitation.

Lynd Morris is the Willow family's other discussion leader. She explains that when Thay talks about a bell of mindfulness, he's referring to more than just a metal instrument. "A bell of mindfulness can be anything that reminds you to come back to yourself," she says. It can be a sound, such as a kettle whistling or a baby crying, but it doesn't have to be. On this retreat, Lynd has been using doorways. Every time she passes through one, she pauses, breathes in and out, and allows the doorway to remind her to say hello to herself and the world around her.

At home, Lynd rings a bell before meals. When she introduced this practice to her children, she described the intent as listening until you could no longer hear the last little bit of vibration. "There was instant focus," she remembers. "It was a kind of game. It was playful."

Thich Nhat Hanh recommends that every family have a bell. It's also helpful, he says, if there's a mini-meditation hall in the house. It can be a whole room or just a corner – all you need is space for a few cushions and maybe a flower. Every morning and evening the family can gather in the mini-meditation hall and invite the bell. They can also invite it whenever the atmosphere in the house is not peaceful.

"Whether you are a child or an adult, you have the right to invite the bell," says Thay. "When you want to cry, when you're irritated, you can go to that small room in your house, invite the bell, and breathe. Maybe Mommy is in the kitchen cutting carrots. When she hears the sound of the bell, she knows that her child is practicing, so she stops cutting carrots and enjoys breathing in and out. And maybe Father is at his desk. He also hears the sound and stops to practice. That is the most beautiful landscape you can see. I think every home in the twenty-first century should have a bell and a mini-meditation hall. That is civilization."

My dharma family's bell is sitting on a red and green cushion shot through with gold thread. When it's my turn to invite, the instrument feels cool in my hand. Breathing in, breathing out, the whole family recites together:

*Body, speech, and mind in perfect oneness, I send my
heart along with the sound of this bell. May those of
you who listen to me awaken from your forgetfulness
and transcend the path of anxiety and sorrow.*

The first time I try to bring the inviter to the bell's lip,
I bring it down too gingerly and miss. I try again and the bell
wakes. Each time I invite the bell, my dharma family says with
me:

*I listen, I listen. This wonderful sound brings me back
to my true home. I listen, I listen. This wonderful
sound brings me back to my true home.*

In his speech "Let Freedom Ring," commemorating the
fiftieth anniversary of the March on Washington, President
Obama has requested that today at three o'clock people across
the country ring bells to proclaim that America still has a dream
to realize.

"The dream of Martin Luther King included civil rights
and jobs," says Thich Nhat Hanh. "But we know we need more
than that. We need peace in ourselves, our family, our nation.

"Today, according to the wish of President Obama, we will
ring a bell, but our way of ringing the bell is a little bit different.
With the bell, we take good care of ourselves and restore peace
inside. We know how to handle a painful emotion, because the
bell helps us go back to our true home. Coming back to ourselves,
to our beloved ones, and to our dear planet Earth – that is the
real dream."

Mindfulness practice helps us cultivate peace in ourselves,
and from that foundation we can engender peace in others. Yet if
we do not have a sangha, our practice can easily grow weak. This
is what Thay emphasizes, as did Martin Luther King: community
is key.

It's after lunch and clouds are gathering. Thick and gray, they make me think of what Thay said during one of his recent dharma talks: the nature of a cloud is no birth and no death.

"When you look into tea, what do you see?" he asked. "I see a cloud. Yesterday the tea was a cloud up in the sky. But today it has become the tea in my glass. When you look up at the blue sky and you don't see your cloud anymore, you might say, 'Oh, my cloud has died.' But in fact, it has not. When I look mindfully into my tea, I see the cloud, and when I drink my tea, I drink the cloud.

"You are made of cloud – at least 70 percent of you," Thich Nhat Hanh continued. "If you take the cloud out of you, there's no you left. A cloud has a good time traveling. When it falls down, it does not die. It becomes snow or rain. The rain becomes a creek, and the creek flows down and becomes a river. The river goes to the sea, then heat generated by the sun helps the water evaporate and become a cloud again. Now the cloud has become tea, and Thay is going to drink it. Then what will become of this tea? It will become a dharma talk."

It might be my imagination, but I think a cloud just manifested into a drop of rain falling on my shoulder. I don't say anything, though, and Peggy Smith and I stay where we are under the imperfect umbrella of a large tree. She has pink cheeks and bobbed hair and is wearing the brown jacket of an Order of Interbeing member, which means she has taken the fourteen mindfulness trainings, or precepts, with Thich Nhat Hanh. She's telling me how she handles a strong, difficult emotion.

"I go through a process of recognizing the reaction in my body," she says. "I assure myself that it's a stormy cloud in the sky and it will pass."

Suddenly, as if on cue, a non-metaphoric cloud breaks open, leaving Peggy and me rushing to take shelter under the dining tent. We settle into chairs and I pose another question: "Thay is always talking about the importance of sangha. How does the sangha support you?"

Her answer, in short, is that it keeps her from being afraid. "For instance," she says, "the day the United States started to bomb Baghdad, there was a group of us who wanted to talk to our senator and express to her our deep disappointment. But her office – the whole building – was locked, so twenty people decided to lay down in the intersection in Portland, Maine. As we approached the intersection, I thought, 'It's March – it's going to be so cold. How am I going to ever do this?' But I lay down and closed my eyes, and Thay was right there. And then the sangha was right behind him. It was one of the best meditations I've ever had in my life. I was so disappointed when the police interrupted it to arrest me!"

I thank Peggy for the interview. With the rain now pelting down on the white tarp above, it's getting difficult to hear her and a crowd is gathering. It is three o'clock, time to let freedom ring.

A stone's throw away, Thay and clutch of people with umbrellas are under a tree inviting the big bell – breathing in, breathing out. We form a messy, accommodating circle under the dining tent that expands into two layers to let everyone in. Line by line, a man reads one of Thay's poems and the rest of us repeat it. We are a powerful human microphone that can be heard even over the thunder:

> *I walk on thorns, but firmly, as among flowers.*
> *I keep my head high.*
> *Rhymes bloom among the sounds of bombs and mortars.*
> *The tears I shed yesterday have become rain.*
> *I feel calm hearing its sound on the thatched roof.*
> *Childhood, my birthland, is calling me,*
> *and the rains melt my despair.*

Rain, tears, tea. The clouds above look interminable, but Thay teaches that they can and do transform. He says, "If you don't practice, you do not know how to handle your suffering and you continue to cry a lot." Yet with mindfulness, tears become rain. New growth follows.

Holding hands, we sing "Amazing Grace." We sing "We Shall Overcome." We sing "Wade in the Water." And for a moment, I have to put my hand over my chest. Like Peggy said, I can feel a strong emotion manifesting in my body. An achy pain, it's half grief over the seemingly endless sorrow of this world. But it's also half joy because here under this tent there is so much love that I think maybe – just maybe – we really will overcome.